# Raising
# Jewish Children
# in a Contemporary
# World

**How to Order:**

Quantity discounts are available from the publisher, Prima Publishing, P.O. Box 1260SC, Rocklin, CA 95677; telephone (916) 786-0426. On your letterhead include information concerning the intended use of the books and the number of books you wish to purchase.

*U.S. Bookstores and Libraries:* Please submit all orders to St. Martin's Press, 175 Fifth Avenue, New York, NY 10010; telephone (212) 674-5151.

# Raising Jewish Children in a Contemporary World

The Modern Parent's Guide to Creating a Jewish Home

Rabbi Steven Carr Reuben, Ph.D.

**Prima Publishing**
P.O. Box 1260SC
Rocklin, CA 95677
(916) 786-0426

Copy editing by Anne Montague
Production by Robin Lockwood, Bookman Productions
Cover design by Kirschner-Caroff Design
Typography by Recorder Typesetting Network

**Library of Congress Cataloging-in-Publication Data**

Reuben, Steven Carr.
    Raising Jewish children in a comtemporary world :
The Modern Parent's Guide to Creating a Jewish
Home / by Steven Carr Reuben.
    p.   cm.
Includes index.
ISBN 1-55958-319-3
    1. Jewish religious education of children.   2. Jewish
way of life.   3. Judaism—Customs and practices.
4. Child rearing—Religious aspects—Judaism.
5. Jewish families—Religious life.   6. Children of
interfaith marriage.   I. Title.
BM103.R44   1992
296.7'4—dc20                    91-30144
                                      CIP

93 94 95 96 RRD 10 9 8 7 6 5 4 3 2

Printed in the United States of America

*This book is dedicated to my parents, Jack and Betty Reuben, who taught me each and every day of my life what it really means to be a successful parent.*

# Contents

# Acknowledgments

This book reflects the combined influences of teachers, friends, colleagues, congregants, and family that stretch back to childhood. It is really impossible to create a comprehensive list of all to whom I owe a debt of gratitude for helping to shape my thoughts, experiences, and perceptions of how Jewish civilization can add a unique and wonderful quality to the lives of Jews and non-Jews alike.

Growing up in a Reform synagogue in Santa Monica, California, where freedom of thought and expression was encouraged and leadership potential in the young was recognized and given wings, showed me that synagogues (even though religious school sometimes did seem "boring") can play an important role in positive identity formation.

To Rabbi Amiel Wohl, who not only encouraged me to become a rabbi, but demonstrated that the title "Rabbi" carried with it both the responsibility and opportunity to be involved in the world beyond the Jewish community.

To all my teachers from religious school to college, from rabbinic school to my doctorate, I thank you for challenging me to think for myself and fashion an understanding of Jewish life that would best serve the emerging needs of a rapidly changing world.

To the leadership and members of my congregation, Kehillath Israel in Pacific Palisades, California, thank you for allowing me the freedom to express myself as I choose. Thank you for the encouragement to further my own continuing education, for understanding my moments of distraction in the midst of writing this book, for welcoming my involvements within the community, both locally and nationally, and for constantly showing me what a dynamic, creative, caring community I have been blessed with. I cannot tell you how much I appreciate the privilege I have of serving as your rabbi.

To Rabbi Allen Freehling, thank you not only for serving for two years as my Ph.D. adviser, but for encouraging me to write this book and introducing me to the wonderful literary agent who made its publication possible. To Leslie Parness, that literary agent who believed, first, in me and, second, that this was an important book, and whose excitement and tears after reading each chapter were a remarkable gift of acknowledgment and support, I am grateful to have found you.

Obviously, the real foundation of my ethics, identity, and understanding of my responsibility to have a positive impact on the world came from my parents, Dr. Jack and Betty Reuben. They have always lived as if they were partners in the process of completing God's creation, and have always encouraged me unconditionally, been my greatest fans and supporters, and made me feel that what I did mattered. They also introduced me to the fundamentals of Reconstructionist thought as it was lived out in the everyday life of our family.

To all my sisters, Ronna, Carolyn, and Debra, for always making me feel special in their eyes and acting like I could be successful at anything I tried. But especially to my sister Carolyn, the real writer in the family, who has been an inspiration and support all my life. Her devotion to excellence is unceasing, her commitment to communicating to her readers ideas that can help transform their lives is unshakable, and the clarity and beauty of her writing serve as a goal that I can only hope one day to approach.

There are no words that could adequately acknowledge the significance of my wife, Didi Carr Reuben, in my life and this book. It was she who constantly urged me to share my approach, my thoughts, my passions with others; she who is my soulmate and partner in everything I do; she who allows my rabbinate to flourish and touches the lives of others with her own selfless devotion to adding joy, love, and blessings into their lives. Someday perhaps I will write a book just about her, and how one person can transform everyone she touches. Her suggestions, thoughtful comments, and influence are everywhere in this book and in my life.

I am grateful to Ben Dominitz of Prima Publishing who first called asking whether I would be willing to take on this particular project, and who with his wife Nancy articulated the questions and concerns that gave shape and urgency to the issues that I subsequently addressed. Thank you for Jennifer Basye and the Prima extended family. Working with her has been a treat that any author would long for.

Thank you to Robin Lockwood of Bookman Productions, who lovingly designed the book itself, and to Anne Montague, whose excellent, thoughtful, and caring editing helped turn my sometimes inelegant manuscript into a text that, I hope, speaks directly to the heart of its readers.

Finally, to my daughter Gable. Though already two years old when she came into my life, she has for nearly a decade brought me untold joy and love, never-ending challenges and excitement, and satisfactions and fulfillment as a parent beyond what I could ever have imagined. She is living proof that one can be a caring, nurturing, thoughtful, loving mensch at any age, and I am proud to be her stepfather and love her with all my heart.

# Introduction

*If the statistics are right, the Jews
constitute but one quarter of one percent of
the human race. . . . Properly, the Jew ought
hardly to be heard of, but he is heard of,
has always been heard of. . . . His
contributions to the world's list of great
names in literature, science, art, music,
finance, medicine, and abstruse learning are
very out of proportion to the weakness of
his numbers.*

*Mark Twain*
**Harper's** *magazine*
*September 1897*

Four thousand years ago, one family set out on a fateful trip from a small town called Ur in ancient Babylonia to an unknown destination. Little did they know that their personal odyssey would result in the founding of the oldest continuous religious civilization on the planet.

Abraham and Sarah (at ages seventy-five and sixty-five, respectively, according to biblical legend) began a search for meaning and purpose in their lives that would end with their descendants wandering the entire face of the globe, from the Middle East to Southeast Asia, Europe to Africa, India to the Americas.

This book is a modest attempt at capturing the essence of the spiritual civilization that succeeding generations of Jews have created for themselves, as they followed in the footsteps of Abraham and Sarah. It strives to provide an easily accessible approach to incorporating those aspects of Jewish heritage, ethics, ritual, and culture that *you* might find meaningful, relevant, and perhaps even inspirational into your life and the lives of your children.

Through the pages of this book, you will discover three key rules for raising Jewishly ethical children, and the three holidays that can help you teach them the most important values of Judaism. You will also come to understand the diverse blending of four thousand years of traditions, customs, holidays, and historical experiences that often makes it difficult for Jews and non-Jews alike to distinguish between the cultural, religious, and ethical components of Jewish civilization.

This book will help you develop a particular perspective on the ethics and culture of Judaism that you will be able to teach in a variety of ways to your children. Can you teach morality without "religion"? Is there a simple formula for transmitting to your children

Jewish identity and a sense of being connected to the Jewish community if you yourself haven't been raised with a lot of Jewish knowledge? Can a non-Jew who has married into the Jewish world still be a partner in transmitting Jewish culture, tradition, and identity to his or her children in an authentic way?

These are just some of the specific questions and concerns that will be addressed. Throughout the book you will find suggestions for creating a personal Jewish lifestyle that can add to the richness and quality of your child-rearing experiences, regardless of your own Jewish background.

This book is designed to serve as a practical guide to raising children with a positive Jewish self-image. It is based on the conviction that to feel emotionally secure and at home with their identity, your children ideally need to understand the most compelling features of their heritage, culture, roots, and ethics.

Parenting experts agree on very little. One thing they all agree on, however, is that your primary role as a parent is to provide your children with strong, positive self-images, a secure sense of their place in the world, and the tools with which to make intelligent, meaningful choices as they grow.

Besides unconditional love and emotional nurturing, successful parenting requires instilling in your children a sense of belonging to a larger community. This book is designed to help in that process of self-discovery, by establishing a connection to the collective history and culture of your people, while providing a roadmap to help you in guiding your children along their own unique journey through life.

I might have titled this book "What Every Jewish Child Should Know About Judaism," for it will reveal what I consider to be the most important ideas, concepts, information, and activities that reflect the key elements of Jewish life. In these pages you will learn the central concepts that underlie Jewish holidays and life-cycle ceremonies, the significance and role of Israel for the Jewish people, what the most important Jewish values are and how to teach them, examples of famous Jews in a variety of fields who can serve as role models and sources of pride for your children, how to deal with the Hanukah/Christmas dilemma, what to tell your children about Judaism and Jesus, and how to encourage them to cherish diversity while feeling secure about their own identity.

You will learn about the key ethical insights of Jewish history and how they transformed all of Western civilization as we know it, as well as how to explain to your child the role that anti-Semitism has played in the Jewish past, and its continued influence on the Jewish psyche.

You will also be reminded of the unusual situation in which we contemporary Jews find ourselves, whereby some Jews call themselves "secular," others "cultural," and others "religious" while possibly meaning exactly the same thing.

This book is written for Jews *and* non-Jews alike. If you are a Jewish parent whose goal is to transmit your heritage, culture, and identity to your children, this book was written for you. If you are a non-Jew married to a Jew with your own desire to understand Judaism and be able to help your children experience their Jewish heritage, you will find this book the perfect vehicle as well. It is written for you regardless of your background, if your goal is to understand the essence of what Judaism is all about, while learning practical, nonjudgmental ways of sharing this knowledge with your children.

Judaism is much more than simply a religion. It is the evolving religious civilization of the Jewish people, and all Jews, no matter how much or little they know about Judaism, share a common historical memory and are linked in common destiny. We are heirs to a rich, vibrant, thriving, exciting, ethical, purposeful, literary, spiritual, and artistic culture and heritage spanning four millennia. This book is one step along your own path to rediscovering that heritage for yourself, and learning how to share it in simple yet powerful ways with your family.

Being a part of the Jewish civilization is like joining an extended family. Just as in a family, one becomes a member either by being born into it, by being adopted into it, or by marrying into it.

Thousands of people each year in North America formally convert to Judaism as adults. This is the equivalent of being adopted into the Jewish family. If you fall into this category, you are what is called a "Jew by choice." There are also tens of thousands of non-Jews who marry Jews each year in North America alone. By marrying into the Jewish family, you become what I like to call a "Jew by association." Very often, Jews by association decide with their Jewish partner to expose their children to Judaism and search for a way to transmit to them a sense of Jewish identity and belonging.

If you are reading this book, you may fall into a third category—those who were born Jewish (to one or more Jewish parents) but have had little connection to Judaism beyond birth, and have learned very little, if anything, about what it means to be Jewish. If this sounds like you, then you are what I call a "Jew by chance."

Chance made you a Jew. Choice can make you whatever kind of Jew you want to be. Choice can also determine the quality of your children's Jewish identity, and the very fact that you picked up this book is a sign that you are taking some measure of control over just those very choices.

There is great diversity within Jewish life. Jews have a wide range of belief, practice, ritual, ceremony, philosophy, and theology. Jews come in all sizes, colors, and genders. There are heterosexual Jews, and there are gay and lesbian Jews. There are Jews who speak Russian and Spanish, Yiddish and Hebrew, Polish and English, Arabic and Chinese. Jews are found in all corners of the world, in all socioeconomic brackets, in all professions embracing all political ideologies.

Whatever your background; however you see yourself as a Jew; whatever your education, both Jewish and secular; whatever your passions and involvements in life, there are other Jews somewhere *just like you*. This book is an introduction to Jewish life that I hope will assist you in reclaiming your own Jewish identity, even while you pass it on lovingly to the next generation.

# One

# Judaism as an Evolving Religious Civilization

*I have never seen a country or a culture
which was not the better for having the
contribution of the Jewish people.*
**Pearl S. Buck**

Judaism is the unique culture of the Jewish people. It is a constantly evolving religious civilization, and like any civilization contains the multiple attributes of language and literature, rituals and customs, art, music, history, ethics, holidays, group hopes and aspirations, and a common spiritual homeland.

Throughout contemporary history, there have been constant attempts at creating a "definition" of Judaism. Since it is a natural human tendency to understand things in relation to what we already know, people generally try to fit Judaism into one or another of the common categories by which other groups within society are defined. That is why, depending on whom you read, Judaism will be referred to as a "religion," a "nationality," a "people," a "culture," a "race," or a "civilization."

In fact, *all* of these labels except for "race" are true. Although Jews were originally Semites from the smallest segment of the Caucasian race, today Jews are found among nearly all races throughout the world, including black, white, and Asian.

## Most Jews Identify
## Primarily with Jewish Culture

It has become almost universally recognized that most Jews experience their identity as Jews primarily through Jewish culture. They feel Jewish when they eat a bagel, gefilte fish, matzah, or potato pancakes. They feel Jewish when they hear Jewish jokes or read stories about Jews, feel a sense of Jewish pride when they listen to Itzhak Perlman play the violin or hear the music of George Gershwin or Leonard Bernstein.

In general, Jews who identify themselves as "cultural" Jews wouldn't describe their behavior or attitudes as

11

being particularly "religious." They generally accept the prevailing stereotype that *religious* is a term referring to those who evidence some form of religious piety and devotion to a supernatural God through prayer.

### What Does It Mean to Be "Religious"?

Yet the very same qualities that many "cultural" Jews cherish in their understanding of Judaism are what others mean when they say they are "religious." For many, *religious* refers to a certain attitude about life, an approach to the world and relationships that validates the highest, noblest, loftiest ideas and ideals of the Jewish people and the process whereby one gives those ideals a voice in one's everyday life.

As I understand the term, people can be called "religious" if they see the world as filled with the opportunity to discover blessings, love, caring, nurturing, compassion, justice, and righteousness. Perhaps we ought to use *religious* to refer to all those who search for higher meaning in life, who believe that human beings are fundamentally created good, endowed with the ability to choose life and joy, wholeness and peace, if only given the chance.

I certainly understand the term *religious* to refer to just such a person. When I see individuals and families who recognize that the most important things in life aren't things at all; when I see parents patiently teaching their children how to distinguish right from wrong, good from bad, caring from neglect, sensitivity from callousness, I describe those individuals as religious, even if they wouldn't use the same term for themselves.

I am reminded of Ralph Waldo Emerson's statement that if the sunset occurred only once every ten years, we would be so awed by it that it would certainly appear to be a miracle. But since it happens every day, we hardly pay any attention to it at all. The soul of a religious person is the one with the vision to remain awed by the sunsets, enchanted by the rain, overjoyed by the laughter of an infant—in short, able to see the miracles that surround us each day.

To me, religion is a broad category that includes the striving to make sense out of the difficult moments of life and the struggle to pass on values that will move the world closer to our collective dreams. Judaism is the result of the particular four-thousand-year march through history of the Jewish people, as each generation struggled to make sense out of the world and then shared the results of that struggle with one another and their children.

That is why I have no trouble calling many people "religious" who see themselves as "cultural." Being religious isn't dependent on the specific rituals, services, ceremonies, holidays, or customs that you celebrate. It is an all-encompassing approach to life, to people, to family, to relationships, and to the future that can be expressed in a wide variety of ways. *Some* of those ways may include the rituals, customs, and holidays that the Jewish people have developed over the thousands of years of our history. But the point isn't the rituals or prayers; it is, rather, the values they symbolize. The rituals are cultural reminders of our most important historical events and ethical values—they are group-building symbols that help bind us together in our identity as members of the Jewish civilization, they are not the essential element in and of themselves.

### Labels Can Be More Harmful Than Helpful

Ultimately, I believe it isn't particularly important what label you attach to people's Jewish identity, whether

"cultural," "religious," or "secular." What *is* important is
how they actually live their lives, the values they strive
to pass on to their children, and the impact they have
on their society as a result of the quality and nature of
the choices they make each day.

Bringing a sense of spirituality into your life and
choosing to fill your life with the symbols of Jewish culture and ethics are aspects of your Jewish identity and
the identity you bequeath to the next generation that
are within your control. My advice to you as you begin
the process of defining your own religious lifestyle and
kind of Jewishness that it will represent is not to worry
about labels, definitions, or what to call the kind of Judaism you are living. It is equally important not to worry about how other people might want to categorize or
define you and your family.

The Judaism you create together, the Judaism that
results from this identity adventure you are sharing, will
undoubtedly fit into one of the many broad categories
by which most Jews define the form of Judaism they
embrace. In Chapter 5 I will briefly outline the identifying elements of the major movements of Judaism in
North America (Reform, Reconstructionist, Conservative, Orthodox), so that when the time comes that you
want to affiliate with a synagogue or the Jewish community in a formal way, you will have a reference point
from which to choose the movement that best fits the
Judaism you have chosen to live.

Other than for the purposes of affiliation and public
identification, however, labels and categories of Jewish
identity are often more divisive than constructive. In a
world where the Jewish people constitute a tiny minority of the population, we would all be better off, stronger
as a community, more united and mutually supportive,

if we emphasized the elements that we have in common, rather than those that divide and fragment us.

Labels tend to isolate, to categorize in broad strokes that leave little room to understand the individual nuances of Jewish identity resulting from the reality of each family's personal Jewish lifestyle choices. People too often say of others, "Oh, they are _____ Jews" (fill in the blank with Reform, Reconstructionist, Conservative, Orthodox, Secular, Humanist, or any other label you choose), as if that single label somehow captures the reality of their Jewish lives.

I know Reform Jews who keep kosher, Reconstructionist Jews who won't ride on the Shabbat, and Conservative Jews who attend morning religious services every day. What separates them isn't easily identifiable to a casual observer, yet too often the labels of Jewish identity are bandied back and forth as if by using the label alone one's entire Jewish life can be understood and defined.

That is why I always warn people away from labels. They are important only to the extent that they help you to identify with a particular philosophy or help in making choices regarding formal affiliation and support for a particular movement or institution. Don't ever allow yourself to be limited by the labels of others.

## Judaism Is How Jews Actually Live

Perhaps above all else, Judaism is simply the way of life of the Jewish people. It defies narrow definition, because Judaism has evolved over the past four thousand years into the totality of the religious strivings, national aspirations, cultural artifacts and rituals, spiritual celebrations, and philosophical ideals that are given expression in the daily lives of Jews throughout the world.

Judaism is the living context within which individual Jews and the Jewish people as a whole work to create meaning and purpose in life. It allows its adherents to articulate the highest ideals of the human spirit, inspiring them to search for answers to the profoundest questions the human heart and mind can confront.

The rich diversity of Jewish practice, ritual, custom, theology, and philosophy that is available to the average Jewish family allows them the flexibility to literally create their own Jewish lifestyle from year to year. Just as Jewish civilization itself is in a constant process of evolution, so, too, each individual Jew and Jewish household fashions their own unique collection of holidays and celebrations, rituals and customs, folkways and traditions through the everyday process of life itself.

So how, then, can you find your way through this maze of often conflicting Jewish traditions and cultural expectations? I am reminded of the book written by the psychiatrist played by Richard Dreyfuss in the movie *What About Bob?* A best-seller designed to help people cope with the overwhelming demands of life, the book is called *Baby Steps*.

Baby steps are exactly what is needed here as well. In order *not* to be overwhelmed by thousands of years of collected Jewish civilization, you have to approach Jewish culture one baby step at a time.

## Your Jewish Inheritance Room

Perhaps this process can best be compared to discovering a hidden attic brimming with treasures from the past that you have inherited. Imagine that at birth, if you were born Jewish, or as an adult, if you came to Judaism by choice, you were given a special key and told that this key was left to you by your ancestors as your inheritance.

This special key unlocks your hidden attic, which is filled with all that Jewish civilization has produced throughout its history. You climb the stairs, put the key in the lock, and open the door. All around you are Jewish artifacts from every country on earth: Seder plates for Passover, candlesticks, wine cups and hallah covers for the Sabbath, dreidels and menorahs for Hanukah, two-thousand-year-old sacred books written in Hebrew and Aramaic, commentaries on the Bible in French and Arabic from the twelfth century, and Yiddish from the eighteenth century, Torah scrolls from Spain, Iraq, Germany, England, Poland, Israel, and Yemen, books of poetry and folktales from around the world, various instruments and music written by Jews in many languages and many styles, every Jewish custom, ritual, ritual object, superstition, holiday, festival, recipe, and costume ever created or practiced by Jews anywhere in the world.

All of this, all four thousand years of Jewish life, is found in your own private attic, and *it all belongs to you.* The things you understand and the things you don't, the rituals you enjoy and the ones that turn you off, the languages that are a total mystery and the holidays that you cherish—every bit of it belongs to you as your Jewish inheritance, whether you ever use any of it or not.

My goal in writing this book, as it is in my work as a rabbi in general, is to convince you that you hold that key in your hand, and it is yours to use as you see fit, forever. Your responsibility as heir to this Jewish cultural fortune is to be willing to unlock the attic on a regular basis, and see what you can discover about the richness of your Jewish inheritance.

There is no way in the world that you will ever understand or grasp all there is to know about everything in the attic. That is, without doubt, an impossible fantasy. What you *can* do, however, is to accept the challenge of constantly updating and expanding your Jewish life skills, knowledge, and cultural competence by being willing to experiment with the vast storehouse of Jewish culture that belongs to you.

The challenge is to see sifting through your Jewish treasure as an exciting lifelong adventure in self-discovery. It is to embrace all that is Jewish as if it were yours, try it on to see how it feels, then decide either to incorporate it into your own emerging Jewish lifestyle, or discard it as not meaningful or relevant for now.

I am reminded of the great twentieth-century Jewish thinker Franz Rosenzweig, who, after standing one Yom Kippur day on the brink of converting to Christianity for the sake of his university career and social expediency, had an unexplained revelation that somehow turned him completely around. (He went on to become one of the greatest Jewish educators, thinkers, and leaders of the past hundred years.) The story is told that one day someone came to Rosenzweig and asked, "Do you keep kosher?" He is reported to have thought for a moment and then replied with all sincerity, "Not yet."

"Not yet" might be your slogan. The important thing isn't whether or not you follow some form of traditional Jewish dietary law, or which particular custom, holiday, or ritual you have incorporated into your life; what is important is the process and your willingness to engage in it.

Creating your own Jewish lifestyle, fashioning your own unique collection of rituals and customs out of the crucible of Jewish history and culture is an exciting and empowering opportunity. It is something you can do together with your entire family, and it can bring you and your spouse and children closer in the most significant of ways.

## Where Does Jewish Culture Come From?

Jewish culture, like the cultures of all other civilizations, emerges from the everyday lives of the people who experience it. Jewish culture comes from you and me, your family and mine, as we pick and choose from the vast resources of the past, and from time to time invent our own special ways of celebrating holidays or sanctifying life and its numerous precious moments.

Jewish culture is a human invention. Born of the ebb and flow of Jewish history, carried from country to country, continent to continent, as our ancestors migrated either voluntarily or by force to create a new life in a new world, Jewish culture steadily grew and evolved.

Unless it is in the process of dying, no culture is ever static. It is an ever-changing, constantly evolving series of rituals and customs, songs and music and poetry, prayers and celebrations that emerges from the daily lives of the people on the streets and in their homes.

## Flexibility and Choices

Part of the greatness of Judaism lies in its ability to adapt itself to the circumstances surrounding it. When Jews lived in Moslem lands, they learned to speak Arabic and copied the architecture of the local mosques as designs for their own synagogues and spiritual centers. When they lived in Europe during the Middle Ages, they borrowed music from the hymns they overheard their Christian neighbors singing in church, and their synagogues imitated Gothic cathedrals.

Judaism has always been blessed with a flexibility that has ensured its survival, growth, and adaptability. I am reminded of an incident reported in the Talmud, the twenty-volume compendium of Jewish law and lore compiled around the year 500 c.e. (common era, the Jewish equivalent of a.d.): A dispute between two distinguished rabbis was settled by saying, "Let's go see what the people are actually doing; for if we follow the customs they have adopted for themselves, we will be making the right choice."

In other words, Jewish tradition placed a very high value on the everyday choices that ordinary Jews made in their own homes regarding how to best live their lives Jewishly. You are empowered every day to participate with your family in the evolution of Jewish civilization. Your choices matter. The rituals you and your family find relevant, inspirational, educational, meaningful, and worth incorporating into your Jewish lifestyle matter. In fact, those very choices that you and millions of others like you make will help form the foundation of Jewish life and practice for the next generation.

Rabbis often quote a famous phrase found several times in the Bible to teach that each of us is responsible for choosing the quality of his or her own life. The version in Deuteronomy (chapter 30, verse 19) reads, "I call heaven and earth to witness this day that I have placed before you life and death, the blessing and the curse; therefore choose life, that both you and your descendants will live."

"Choosing life" in Jewish tradition is a term that refers to choosing that which enhances the quality of your life, which brings greater meaning and purpose to your life and enriches it. It also clearly sends the message that your choices affect not only your own life but the lives of your children and through them future generations as well. That is why Judaism is fundamentally a religious civilization and culture that empowers the individual. It assumes that each of us has both the right and the power to determine our own destiny and chart our own cultural course.

The truth is, we *must* choose. It's in the very nature of life itself. It is by choosing that we assert our own uniqueness as individuals in the midst of what often seems an overwhelming sea of impersonal humanity. Choices set us apart from others, even as they help connect us to a particular culture or group. By choosing to act in a way that other members of a particular cultural group act, you are asserting your membership in that group.

## Developing Your Own Understanding of Jewish Culture

So how do you develop your own understanding of Judaism? In a sense, you create it each time you choose to celebrate a holiday or participate with your family in a Jewish ritual. In other words, the best way for you to understand the *cultural* component of Judaism is simply by participating in aspects of Jewish culture. It is exactly the same for your children as well. Children learn about Jewish culture in only one way: by living it.

For example, if you want your children to appreciate and identify with Jewish culture, you must seek out opportunities for them to participate in activities, groups, and experiences that are clearly Jewish in nature. Subscribing to a Jewish newspaper in your community will provide valuable information about the wide range of Jewish opportunities available to you and your family.

"Jewish culture" is that aspect of Jewish life that expresses itself through art and music, prose and poetry, movies, plays, food, language, dance, and attitudes about life. An identity based on Jewish culture is one in which your primary focus is on the cultural components of Judaism, as experienced first in your home, and then out in the community.

Look around your home. Would a stranger who walked from room to room know it's a Jewish home? What are the cultural symbols of Judaism that adorn your walls, your bookshelves, your mantel? Is there art that reflects Jewish culture or tradition? Can Jewish ritual objects be found—a menorah, a kiddush cup, Shabbat candlesticks, a Seder plate? Is there a mezuzah on any of the doors of your house? Are books about Jewish history, culture, and religion displayed and read in your home?

These cultural symbols are daily reminders of a Jewish identity and consciousness, and their absence is as powerful a message to everyone who lives in or visits your home as their presence. Establishing a Jewish cultural environment is a step-by-step process, and the first step is as simple as paying attention to the external symbols of Judaism in your home that are in your power to create.

The goal is for your children to live in an environment that is Jewishly nurturing. You want to create a home that in a variety of ways communicates both overt and subliminal messages to your children that being Jewish is something to be proud of. This process is relatively simple to begin, requiring only your own commitment to bringing Jewish culture into the life of your family. The key is your willingness to begin filling your life and the lives of your children with Jewish cultural artifacts, one step at a time.

### Bringing Jewish Culture into Your Life, One Step at a Time

Creating a Jewish cultural environment doesn't happen overnight. It takes time to find those elements of Jewish culture that are compatible with your own internal needs, beliefs, and values. It takes time to become familiar with the options that are available to you, and to find out which from all these many choices best fit into your own unique family lifestyle.

Creating a Jewish cultural environment is, in a sense, a lifelong experiment. Ideally, you can see it as an adventure in identity that you will share with your spouse and your children. It is a process whereby you are encouraged to remain open to the possibility of incorporating new aspects of the totality of Jewish civilization into the fabric of your daily life.

Usually, the greatest problem is simply knowing where and how to begin. It is the fear of being overwhelmed by thousands of years of Jewish history and civilization and not feeling certain about how to take the first step that cause so many to experience a form of cultural paralysis.

One of the most important lessons you can learn is that it is practically impossible to do it wrong. Jews all over the world approach Jewish culture in so many different ways, you will find ample validation for almost *any* choices you might make.

The single most important step is to become willing to choose in the first place. The very act of making a decision to *do* something about creating a nurturing Jewish cultural environment for your children can inspire you to realize that you *can* in fact have mastery over your own cultural destiny.

*What's Right for You Is the Right Choice*

Pick any area of *your* interest first. For example, you might start with finding something to do as a family on Shabbat (the Jewish Sabbath, from Friday night to Saturday night) that somehow makes it different from the rest of the week.

Obviously, many Jewish families celebrate Shabbat by reciting or singing blessings over the candles, wine, and bread (hallah), but this is by no means the only acceptable way to celebrate the cultural contribution that the Sabbath can bring into your life. I will go into some detail about Shabbat as a weekly opportunity to make Judaism a special part of your home and your children's lives in Chapter 3, so I use it here only as an example of what might be done.

You might pick a favorite family experience that you all love to do together and incorporate that activity into your regular Shabbat observance. It might be going to a local museum, walking along the beach, hiking into the mountains, going on a family picnic, taking a drive into the country, paying a visit to a relative or friend, going to the hospital just to bring cheer to lonely patients, taking time for everyone to read a good book or study something out of the ordinary, or read part of the weekly portion of the Torah to one another at home.

Any of these activities and a hundred more that you and your family might come up with need only one thing in common: creative thinking. The important element that they all share is that they help you set the

Shabbat apart from the rest of the week, and make it "extra"-ordinary.

### Ritual Creates a Sense of Belonging

People who light candles or participate in any of the other traditional rituals for Friday night often tell me that the act makes them feel connected to Jews throughout the world because they know that other Jews are doing exactly the same thing. Indeed, creating this sense of belonging to a greater community is one of the most important benefits of participating in any ritual, custom, or holiday.

As you can see, creating the cultural component of Judaism within your own family is as simple as making choices throughout the year that will add new and interesting Jewish experiences to your family's lifestyle. It is less important how many you add each year, or even which choices you make. The key is simply the willingness to experiment and involve your family in the process of choosing.

With small children of preschool age, obviously the choices will be primarily up to you. Once your children are elementary school age and older, you can allow them more and more opportunities to make choices from among alternatives that you present to them.

For example, children of all ages can share in preparing and eating Jewish foods, like the twisted egg-bread (hallah) on Friday nights, potato pancakes (latkes) and jelly doughnuts (a custom from Israel) on Hanukah, apples and honey (for a sweet year) on the Jewish New Year (Rosh Hashana), and matzah on Passover. Furthermore, plenty of Jewish books and magazines, groups and organizations, both locally and nationally, can give you ideas for possible rituals and cultural customs that you might want to include as part of your family routine. These and other resources to help you with your child raising and Jewish family life decisions are listed at the end of this book in Chapter 7.

*It's OK to Start Small*

How do you create a Jewish cultural lifestyle when you don't have a solid Jewish background or education? One small step at a time. Start with one thing that you are willing to add to your family life this week. Don't be overzealous and try to incorporate too many new things all at once. You will overwhelm yourself and your family, and quickly feel frustrated and in over your head. Better to "make haste slowly," as a friend of mine always says, so that each time you add something you are already at home and comfortable with what has gone before.

*Any* thing that you add in the beginning feels like a major step, because it is. Remember that more important than the actual choices you make is the fact that you are making choices and slowly adding to the richness of your cultural experiences. Everything worthwhile takes time to build—so too with a cultural identity.

For your children to feel at home with new rituals, new foods, new traditions that you are introducing into their lives, they need time to try them on for size and break them in. The first time you do most things, they feel a bit awkward, artificial, or even forced. But by the third or fourth time you have done the same thing, it begins to seem like you've always done it, and can't imagine doing it any other way.

It is also easier to get comfortable with activities that you can do every week, as opposed to holidays, which come only once a year. Lighting candles on Hanukah and saying the traditional blessings over the lights and the miracle of the successful struggle for religious freedom that the holiday represents will inevitably seem awkward at first. Since the holiday is eight days long, the words of the blessings may begin to feel a bit more familiar by the end of the week, but you won't have another chance to recite them for an entire year.

By the time Hanukah rolls around a year later, you may very well feel awkward all over again at the beginning. The difference will be that the next year, you will have the added self-confidence of having already successfully added the ritual of lighting candles and saying the blessings to your family's cultural repertoire and it will be that much easier to do. By the next year, everyone in your family will have come to expect that you eat latkes, light candles, say the blessings, and anything else that you choose to add to your own particular form of celebrating the holiday.

### There Is Always More Than One "Right" Way

Even though the holiday blessings, for example, were originally recited in Hebrew, and are recited to this day in Hebrew by Jews of all persuasions throughout the world, it is perfectly acceptable to say them only in English as well. The point is for you to find the formula that works best for *you*, not to feel that if you don't do something the "traditional" way then it somehow doesn't count. In fact, even in the most traditional of Jewish legal sources, the Talmud, the rabbis state that it is always more important for you to perform a particular ritual or recite the prayer than it is to worry about the particular language you use to do it.

There isn't only one "right" way to do just about anything in Jewish life, unless you are a Jewish fundamentalist (usually called an Orthodox Jew). There are lots of right ways, hundreds of variations, innumerable opportunities for you and your family to add your own unique voice to the chorus of Jewish culture. Don't let anyone tell you that *his or her* way is the only right way, and *your* way is wrong. The very strength and vitality of Jewish life throughout the generations can be directly attributed to the flexibility and creativity of individual Jews and their families, as they adapted Jewish rituals, customs, holidays, ceremonies, and celebrations to meet the needs of their own particular life situations.

As I will remind you often in the pages of this book, Judaism was created for you, not the other way around. It is a civilization that has evolved over the past four thousand years because of Jewish families just like yours (including interfaith families), from all kinds of backgrounds in countries throughout the world. Each individual, each family, each community has added its own particular version of celebrating, of marking special moments, of signaling to themselves and others that their Jewish heritage has a richness and depth that adds something special to their lives.

All of them, like you, were doing their best to fill their lives with meaning and purpose. Each of us wants to feel that who we are and what we add to the world somehow make a small difference in the total quality of human life on our planet. In the end, *that* is really what Jewish civilization, culture, religion, and ethics are all about. Your contribution, your choices are just as valid and important as the contributions of any other Jews at any other time in history. Don't let anyone tell you differently.

## Your Choices Are Practically Limitless

Part of the greatness of contemporary Jewish life is the unending expanse of options available to each and every Jew, no matter what they call themselves. Your choices are practically limitless, and the realization that you have the ability to choose just about any way you want to celebrate your Jewish life, create your own Jewish home traditions, and draw upon the entire four thousand years of Jewish history and culture as a primary resource can be one of the most exciting discoveries of your life.

# Two

# How to Raise Ethical Jewish Children

*The pursuit of knowledge for its own sake,
an almost fanatical love of justice, and the
desire for personal independence—these are
the features of the Jewish tradition which
make me thank my stars that I belong to it.*
                                    *Albert Einstein*

Jews are proud of the fact that their heritage, culture, and religion stretch back over four thousand years. There is a tremendous sense of rootedness in knowing that the values we espouse, the rituals that have been passed down, and the literature we read and study weren't invented yesterday, but have stood the test of time. In fact, the need to be grounded in a solid tradition of ethics, values, and culture is what often draws non-Jews to investigate Judaism. Our world is fragmented and unstable, people are frightened and insecure. The ability to turn to an ancient tradition for guidance and wisdom in times of stress and moral searching clearly resonates with a fundamental need of the human psyche.

Yet for many, the very fact that Judaism spans thousands of years of history makes it seem all the more forbidding and out of reach. People often shake their heads and tell me they would really *like* to have a better understanding of what Judaism is all about (particularly modern Judaism), but it just seems so daunting. "How could I possibly have the time to *begin* to take in all that I would have to read in order to gain even the vaguest idea of what Judaism has taught?" they lament.

To study thousands of years of anyone's history would take more than a lifetime, and plenty of scholars and interested individuals do study the Jewish religion, culture, and heritage as a lifetime pursuit. But this book is designed to allow you in a few chapters to grasp the essence of that which makes Judaism what it is, and to develop the skills and tools to pass that essence along to your children.

The one aspect of Jewish culture and tradition that holds the highest priority for most parents is the question of how they can successfully pass on an under-

33

standing of Jewish ethics to their children. That is why in this chapter you will learn about the three most important Jewish ideas that have subsequently shaped all of Western civilization. These concepts will serve as guideposts to help you along the path to raising Jewishly ethical children. I have chosen these three ideas because they represent the essence of Jewish ethics and values, and they have inspired countless generations of Jews and non-Jews throughout the world.

## Take the Bible Seriously
## Without Taking It Literally

So what are these magical ideas that have sustained such power and impact over all these centuries? Since the Bible is the best-selling book of all time, it's no surprise that they are found within its pages. Now before you are turned off (as many are) by the very idea of reading anything from the Bible, let me share with you one of my favorite ideas from Dr. Mordecai Kaplan, one of the most influential Jewish thinkers of the twentieth century and founder of Reconstructionist Judaism (which happens to be my own particular orientation).

Kaplan recognized decades ago that modern scientific rules for examination and discovery of how the world actually works and where ancient literature really comes from would make the old-time beliefs in the Bible as a "divinely revealed book" impossible to accept for the contemporary Jew. At the same time, he recognized that the stories in the Bible, the "sacred myths" of the Jewish people, as it were, are filled with powerful lessons, morals, and truths that continue to stand the test of time.

The modern challenge, as Kaplan put it, is for contemporary Jews like us to learn how to take the Bible *seriously* without having to take it *literally*. To approach it seriously doesn't mean you must read it as if it were intended to be a factual account describing exactly who said what to whom, how many years someone spent in a particular location, or what words a Divine Being spoke to Abraham, Isaac, Sarah, or Moses.

It *does* mean that when we read the stories each year, we can discover our own meaning within them, learn a little about the ancient culture from which all modern forms of Judaism have emerged, and find important lessons that reflect the entire range of normative human behavior and teach about everyday life situations—about blended families, sibling rivalry, justice, compassion, and making the world a place we all want to live in.

So we turn to the Bible, but not because we must believe it to be a divinely inspired document dictated by a God in heaven to Moses on the top of Mount Sinai, then passed down faithfully from generation to generation as the literal pronouncement from on high. I don't believe that and neither do most of the Jews I encounter in our modern world. Instead, we turn to the Bible because of the beauty of its prose and poetry, the loftiness of its ideals, the inspiration to be found in its powerful ethical calls for justice and equality, dignity of the human spirit, compassion for the homeless, the orphan, the downtrodden, the poor.

We turn to the Bible because contained within its pages are words and ideas that have formed the very foundation of ethics and morality for our entire Western civilization for the past three millennia. Some of it is archaic and woefully out of date, of course. But the essential spirit of Judaism, those values that all of us hope to pass along to our children and our children's children, had their beginnings in the biblical texts that

emerged out of the historical encounters of the Jewish
people with the world around them.

## What Judaism Really Means By "Holy"

The first of the three most important ideas in Judaism
is found in Leviticus, the third book of the Bible. (The
first five books of the Bible, called "The Five Books of
Moses," are Genesis, Exodus, Leviticus, Numbers, and
Deuteronomy. These are also collectively called the Torah.) If you ever want to glance through the Bible in
search of pearls of wisdom, the best place to start is with
chapter 19 of Leviticus. Jewish tradition called it the
"Holiness Code," because it contains the most concise
prescription ever written for how to create a society that
reflects the Jewish ideal of holiness.

When I use the term *holiness* with most non-"religious" Jews, they inevitably have visions of pious, ascetic
men and women engaged in spiritual meditation and
prayer, striving for communion with a divine supernatural power.

But Judaism has never seen holiness primarily in
such otherworldly terms. To be "holy" in Judaism
means to act in such a way as to bring our highest and
noblest ideals and values into play in our everyday lives.
It isn't about mystic meditation, it's about clothing the
naked, housing the homeless, caring for the elderly and
frail, treating people with dignity and compassion and
justice. *That's* holiness for Jews.

Now, you don't just have to take my word for it.
That's why I'm quoting the Bible in the first place—so
you will realize that this idea of "holiness" as a function
of correct moral behavior is as old as Judaism itself.

Chapter 19 of Leviticus contains a fabulous list of
the various responsibilities we have toward other hu-

man beings; if we each acted on these "commandments" and taught them to our children, the world would be the kind of place we all dream of living in. For example, it commands us to leave a part of our harvest for the poor and the stranger within our midst, to teach that all we own doesn't belong only to us—a portion of it *by right* belongs to those in need.

## Charity versus Tzedakah (Righteousness)

From this biblical passage we get the Jewish idea that "charity" is not merely a voluntary offering of goodwill, something that flows out of the goodness of our hearts alone. In Jewish tradition, giving to those in need is an *obligation* of being human. It *is* what being "religious," being "holy," is all about. We must give to the less fortunate not simply because we *feel* like it this week, but because it is the right thing to do. The English word *charity* has its root in the Latin *caritas*, which is a form of love. Charity, then, in Christian tradition is an act done by one human being to another as a reflection of the love we are supposed to feel toward other people. But what if we *don't* feel particularly loving today, or any given day? That's why Judaism doesn't rely on the vagaries of human love to ensure that those in need are taken care of.

The Jewish substitute for charity is the Hebrew term *tzedakah*, which comes from the root meaning "justice." In Judaism, we take care of those in need *regardless* of how we feel about them, simply because it is just to do so.

It reminds me of my favorite scene from the Broadway musical *Fiddler on the Roof*. The town beggar approaches Tevye the milkman and asks for a contribution. When Tevye gives him two kopeks, the beggar says, "But last week you gave me *four* kopeks!" Tevye replies, "Yes, but I had a bad week," to which the beggar retorts with righteous indignation, "Just because *you* had a bad week, why should *I* suffer?"

For the Jew who takes biblical ethics seriously, supporting those poorer than us is not really a matter of choice at all—it is a moral and ethical ("religious") obligation. In fact, Jewish tradition tells us that even those who receive charity are required to give charity to those poorer than themselves. That's how pervasive this notion of universal obligation and responsibility is in Jewish life, and how seriously it is taken.

I vividly recall as a young man hearing my mother explain the ethical commandments of the Bible in practical, everyday terms. She said that since chapter 19, verse 13, of Leviticus tells us, "The wages of a hired servant shall not abide with you all night until the morning," the "Jewish thing to do" is to make sure that each week when the housekeeper came to clean our house, she got paid that same day. To me, this was a lesson that being Jewish required me to treat other people in certain ways that were just, right, and ethical.

## Love Your Neighbor as Yourself

As I mentioned before, chapter 19 of Leviticus contains the first of my "top three" most important Jewish ideas. It is found in the middle of verse 18, and I am sure you already know it, since it is without doubt one of the most famous verses in all the Bible. It reads simply, " . . . you shall love your neighbor as yourself."

"Love your neighbor as yourself" in the example I just mentioned meant that just as I would expect to be paid promptly for work that I might do, and would see it as an element of being treated with dignity and respect, so, too, I must treat others in the same way. It was a practical lesson in loving my neighbor, and I never forgot it.

"Love your neighbor as yourself." Sounds fairly simple, yet it is one of the most sophisticated notions of biblical ethics. The obvious meaning of the text seems to command us to extend love to our neighbors. But the understated zinger in these simple five words is that to love your neighbor as yourself, first *you have to love yourself.*

Have you ever been on an airplane and listened as the flight attendant ran through the emergency procedures before the flight? You are instructed that in the event of a sudden loss of cabin pressure, oxygen masks will drop down from the ceiling in front of your seat. The attendant then says, "If you are traveling with small children, place the oxygen mask on *yourself first,* then put the masks on your children." Just as you must put the mask on yourself first before you can effectively take care of anyone else in an airplane emergency, so too must you be able to extend love to yourself, before you are fit to demonstrate love for another human being.

"Loving another as yourself" implies that you love yourself. Every psychologist and psychiatrist I have ever spoken with has affirmed the fact that individuals who are incapable of loving themselves, of nurturing feelings of positive self-worth and value, are equally incapable of truly expressing love for anyone else.

### The Importance of Self-Esteem

Your primary task as a parent is to fill up your child's inner reserve of self-worth so full that it will last a lifetime. A solid and secure sense of their own value and place in the world is an essential component of your children's long-term emotional well-being.

What, then, are the implications for child rearing contained in the "Love your neighbor as yourself" idea? First, it is important for you to realize as a parent that teaching your children to love themselves does not imply that they will be selfish, egotistical, self-centered, ill-mannered, spoiled, or demanding. All of these come from spoiling your children by withholding the kind of structure, discipline, and limits they desperately need, and by overindulging their whims and desires.

To grow up as fully functioning, emotionally mature adults, your children need the strong foundation of self-esteem that only you can provide. Part of this self-esteem will grow out of specific experiences in which they see themselves as expressing love for others. In fact, it is primarily through such experiences of loving others in concrete, identifiable ways that we reinforce our own self-worth and value as caring human beings. Let us look at some specific examples of just how this process works.

### "Loving Your Neighbor" in Action

First, you might take your children with you to volunteer at a local soup kitchen or homeless shelter. At almost any age, children have a natural compassion for others (especially other children) who are in need. Children have a built-in sense of fairness and justice. In fact, the complaint from our children we parents hear most frequently are the three little words "It's not fair!" Kids want life to be fair, and are constantly frustrated by the discovery that it isn't.

So kids know what you are talking about when you speak of fairness. They know that it isn't fair for little kids to be homeless; it isn't fair for little kids to be hungry. It isn't fair for little kids to go without nice clothes, or things to play with, or friends. You will constantly be surprised by the depth of passion your children will feel for the plight of others.

### Gable and the Ethiopian Famine

A number of years ago when my daughter Gable was five years old, she happened to see a television story about a famine in Ethiopia. The screen was filled with images of families with young children, in rags, who were starving in poor villages and refugee camps.

At the end of the report, without a word to me or her mother, Gable quietly went into her room. About fifteen minutes later she emerged with an enormous bag filled to the brim with her clothes, and an envelope with $11.32. "These are for the Ethiopian children," she resolutely announced. You can be sure that the very next day we took her with us to an organization that had taken on the responsibility for sending clothes and other needed items to help ease the Ethiopian famine.

At the age of five, Gable had already internalized some of the values her mother and I had been expressing through our own actions in many other settings that Gable had witnessed. I had been one of a few individuals in our community responsible for starting a homeless shelter that year, so Gable had been exposed often to our conversations about our responsibility to help others.

"Love your neighbor as yourself" was not an idle phrase in our household. It was something expressed in our day-to-day lives in the most physical, concrete, and identifiable ways. The next year we took Gable with us to the children's ward of a local hospital during the

Christmas/Hanukah season, and had her give little holiday gifts to the kids. She loved being able to brighten their day with these simple gifts, and it taught her an indelible lesson in "loving your neighbor."

Ever since that time, we have taken her with us periodically to the local homeless shelter with bags of clothes or food donations we have collected through my synagogue. You can do the same thing in your own home, in your own community, with or without an affiliation with a religious institution. Organize a food or clothing drive at your child's school, and your children will learn not only that loving your neighbor is important to you, but that it ought to be important to them as well.

Children learn what they live, plain and simple. There are few claims in life more devastating than the one leveled at parents, teachers, or religious leaders that we teach one standard and live another. Children can spot the truth every time. You can't fool them. If you want to teach your children that to be a good Jewish human being (or any other kind of human being), you must love others and show them compassion, caring, and concern, you must live those values yourself. Your children will emulate what you do, and won't pay much attention to what you say (in case you haven't noticed by now) unless it is consistent with your own behavior.

So how do you teach the concept "Love your neighbor" to your children? It isn't through trying to nurture warm and caring *feelings* or lofty and grandiose *thoughts* about how wonderful your neighbors might be. It is, rather, directly reflected in the *actions* you take that demonstrate your compassion for others. No one really knows what goes on in anyone else's mind and heart. Your children can never really tell how you or anyone else truly feels about anything. What they *can* know is what you *do* about the world around you.

As the primary role model for your children, you will determine what they integrate into the emotional center of their lives as right or wrong, important or unimportant, necessary or useless, functional or dysfunctional when it comes to how they perceive and treat other people.

In my office I have a framed quotation on the wall which reads simply, "Caring for people is our only business." Gable sees that quote every time she walks into my office (which is often), and she sees a hundred different ways in which Didi (her mother) and I get involved in helping others with the problems of their lives. Didi has been constantly creating new organizations and volunteering to serve on local committees to work with estranged youth in the community, bring parents and children together, or fulfill other important social needs. One byproduct of all this is that Gable *sees* that helping other people is simply part of our everyday lives.

On our kitchen counter is a beautiful ceramic box, called a tzedakah box. As I mentioned earlier, *tzedakah* literally means "righteousness" in Hebrew, and it refers to that quality of social responsibility that I have been discussing. Our tzedakah box is a loose change catchall, in which we save money to be given to worthwhile causes.

In our house on Friday night before we recite the traditional prayers over candles, wine, and bread and go to services (I *am* a rabbi, after all), each of us puts some money in the tzedakah box. It reminds us that even while we are privileged to celebrate the Sabbath in peace, freedom, health, and well-being, the world is filled with others who are not so fortunate. It is also a

subtle reminder that as Jews, we link holiness, and turning inward spiritually (like saying prayers on the Sabbath), with actions that are directed outward toward
improving the lives of others.

In fact, Jewish tradition teaches us that no synagogue or place of worship is kosher unless it has at
least one window in it, so we will always remember that
what goes on *inside* the synagogue (like reciting prayers)
is meaningful only if it inspires those who do it to go
*outside* the synagogue and make the world a better
place. The prayers are not ends in themselves, they are
merely means to the real ends. Prayers are seen as en-
abling activities, inspirational experiences that can remind the one who is reciting them of what our real
values are all about.

Jewish prayers speak of healing the sick, freeing the
captive, raising the downtrodden, and bringing peace
into the world. They do so in order that *we* will remember that all those things can come about only if each of
us plays a part in making them happen. In the end, our
children will learn that one of the most important of all
Jewish values is "Love your neighbor as yourself" only
to the degree that we ourselves demonstrate what such
loving behavior is all about.

### Hillel's Golden Rule

One of the best known of all ethical standards of behavior started with a rabbi named Hillel in Israel about two
thousand years ago. The famous story is told of a pagan
who came to the great Hillel and said he would become a
Jew if Hillel could teach him the entire Torah (specifically the five books of Moses, but also a term used to refer
to Jewish law in general) while standing on one foot.

Rather than become annoyed with what was probably meant as ridicule, Hillel is said to have calmly and lovingly replied, "What is hateful to you, do not unto your neighbor: this is the entire Torah. All the rest is commentary—now go and study it."

Many of you may be more familiar with this phrase as it was retold by Hillel's most famous student, who is quoted in the New Testament book of Matthew as saying, "Do unto others as you would have others do unto you." This is the famous "Golden Rule" of Jesus, who scholars think probably studied under Hillel, since many of the aphorisms attributed to him in the Gospels of the New Testament are actually simple reformulations of Hillel's teachings.

"What is hateful to you, do not unto your neighbor" is a formula for loving your neighbor as yourself. It is even more inclusive a statement than the Golden Rule formulation, since it is directed at the other and not at the self. Avoiding acting in any way that you yourself would find unacceptable is the simplest way possible to establish a foolproof system of proper ethical behavior.

Telling someone "Do unto others as you would have them do unto you" may be construed as asking for self-centered, even selfishly motivated ethical behavior. It is essentially giving people permission to first decide what *they* want, and then act toward others in that way in the hopes that others might reciprocate in kind.

### The "How Would I Like It?" Rule

How should you translate Hillel's rule for a child? I have often told Gable that the easiest measure of her own behavior in almost any circumstance is the "How would I like it if the situation were reversed?" test.

Whenever she has any question whatsoever concerning the appropriateness of her behavior, all she has to do is imagine that the tables were turned, and the other person was acting toward her as she is toward him or her. If that would be OK with her, then her behavior is probably OK as well. If she wouldn't like to have whatever she is doing done to her, than it's a pretty good bet that she shouldn't be doing it to anyone else either.

"What is hateful to you, do not unto your neighbor" is another ethical standard by which we can measure how well we are living out Most Important Jewish Idea #1, "Love your neighbor as yourself." If we are behaving in a way that is consistent with Hillel's famous admonition of the Golden Rule, then we can be fairly certain we are doing a passable job of living the commandment to love our neighbor as ourselves.

If you use these rules to set guidelines and standards for your children, you will be handing down to them the most important ideals and values that have grown out of the thousands of years of Jewish ethics, history, and culture. By laying this crucial ethical foundation for them early in their lives, you will have gone a long way toward fulfilling your essential parental obligation of raising your children to be caring, compassionate, ethical, loving human beings.

## The Primary Goal of Humanity

Most Important Jewish Idea #2 was developed by the rabbis of the Talmud (a word that means "instruction"). The Talmud is the collection of stories, laws, anecdotes, arguments, commentaries, and discussions that the rabbis carried on concerning every aspect of life in their community over a three-hundred-year period from about 200 to 500 C.E. It is from the Talmud and its discussions that most of contemporary Jewish law, custom, ritual, and ethics trace their roots.

Contained in the twenty volumes that comprise the Talmud are some of the loftiest, most inspirational and socially demanding ideas in all the history of Western civilization. It's not surprising, then, that the second most important Jewish idea is a concept found in the Talmud, since it is here that the rabbis formulate the primary goal of humanity.

What is the primary goal of humanity? It is to join as partners in completing the work of creation. It shouldn't surprise you that Judaism, as a religious tradition, teaches that *God* is the term we use to refer to that power that is the source of creation in the universe. That power, which is clearly greater than you or I, which animated all life in the beginning and continues to renew creation on a daily basis, needs us to finish its work, according to Jewish tradition.

### The Challenge of "Fixing the World"

Our job is what is called in Hebrew *tikun olam*. It literally means "fixing the world." We are challenged with the task of repairing this broken world of ours (and certainly no one would argue that it is intact), and bringing it ever closer to the ultimate goal of wholeness and peace.

You are probably familiar with the Hebrew term *shalom*. Most people think *shalom* means "peace," because that is the easiest way to translate it. In fact, *shalom* comes from a Hebrew root that means "wholeness" or "completeness." "Peace" in Jewish tradition has very little to do with the cessation of conflict or declaring a cease-fire between opposing forces in a war.

Peace as shalom is an active, positive state that involves total well-being, wholeness of spirit and mind, safety, security, and a life of calm and contentment. It is not the absence of war, it is the creation of a state in which we feel at one with the world and integrated within the social fabric of society.

## Jews as Overachievers

*Tikun olam* decrees that our primary task as human beings is to do whatever we can in our lifetime to bring shalom into the world. We are to repair the fragments of the world we live in—mend the shattered lives around us; bring comfort to the sick at heart; bring healing to the sick of body; bring shelter to the homeless; bring food to the starving; bring clothes to the ragged; bring hope to those in despair.

It is really a tall order, if you ask me, and it probably accounts for the unreasonably high percentage of achievers in all fields of endeavor among this tiny population in the world called Jews. According to Molly Cone, the author of *The Mystery of Being Jewish* (1989), the theory of relativity, the science of psychoanalysis, cybernetics, holography, neurophysiology, bacteriology, chemotherapy, vitamins, and the polio vaccine were all discovered or developed by Jews.

With only 3 percent of the population of the United States, Jews account for 27 percent of the Nobel Prizes awarded American scientists. Jews are overrepresented in medicine by 231 percent in proportion to the general population, in psychiatry by 478 percent, in dentistry by 299 percent, and in mathematics by 238 percent. That's a lot to be proud of.

As a parent who wants your children to be proud of who they are, their roots, their heritage, their people, you can point to these and many other accomplishments, which in and of themselves can inspire a great sense of purpose and pride among Jews of all ages. *Tikun olam*, fixing the world, is a lifelong task for all of us. Yet the road to its accomplishment is deceptively easy— it lies in simply being the best *us* that we can be.

### Being the Best "Us" We Can Be

Without question, one of the greatest realizations any child can be blessed with is that with all the billions of human beings on earth, she is one of a kind. There never has been in all the millions of years of the world's history, and there never will be in the future, another human being exactly like her. She is unique, the only "her" that will ever be, and as such her task while she is on this beautiful earth is to simply be the best "her" she can possibly be.

Too often our children shed tears of grief, longing to be someone else, wondering why they aren't the girl down the block who always seems so popular, or the boy next door who is star quarterback on the football team, or the kid in their class who always gets the A's on every test, and so on, and so on. They struggle to be someone else, never realizing that, try as they might, they will never be able to be better than their idol, even if that idol isn't so special to begin with.

At the same time, no matter how hard someone else may try to be like them, *they* will always do it better—no matter what. That is why being yourself, just being the best *you* can possibly be, is the most important challenge in life. You are the only one who can do it.

Successful parenting involves communicating to your children that they can make a difference in the world. It requires them to discover, with your help, that with all the problems afflicting our world, with all the pain and suffering, all the sorrow and grief, all the struggles and frustrations, *they* can bring more light, joy, and love into even the darkest corner.

### Teaching the Meaning of Life

Your children don't have to be famous inventors, scientists, athletes, entertainers, or political figures to accomplish the most important things in life. After all, your job is to teach your children that the most important things in life aren't things at all. They are found in the quiet moments of caring and love that pass between lovers, friends, parents and children, teachers and students.

Touching the world, fixing the world, is possible for everyone, for it is the most important reason for being alive. In Judaism, the meaning of life is found in reaching out to others. Jews reject the isolation of living for oneself alone, in favor of the responsibilities that come with being part of a community, a people, and a family.

*Tikun olam* means experiencing your life as connected with the lives of all other human beings. It means feeling responsible for the quality of life on our planet, the quality of the air we breathe, the water we drink, the food we eat, the well-being of our society as a whole, and the fate of humanity on this little planet.

Teaching *tikun olam* is both challenging and exciting. It takes place in the simple gestures, the ordinary moments of life. Our task is to teach our children that when they look back on their lives, they will realize that the most important things were not written large in the bold print of headlines but were found in the small print of their everyday encounters with each human being who crossed their path.

Teaching your children that it is our responsibility together to do whatever we can to create a world that nurtures, supports, and sustains everyone in dignity and well-being requires the same type of concrete behavior necessary to teach the idea of loving your neighbor as yourself.

We engage in *tikun olam*, fixing the world, each time we do our part to right a wrong, to bring more justice, caring, compassion, and dignity into the lives of others. You might ask your children "What do you think is wrong with the world?" Then list on a piece of paper all the things they come up with.

After your list is done (you can always go back and add to it later), write each entry on the top of a single page of paper. Next, have a family brainstorming session with parents and children, in which you take one problem at a time and think of as many different and creative ideas as you can for fixing the problem. The more inventive and unusual the better, for it helps all of you to break out of the easy-to-think-of, ordinary solutions to these important issues.

Go through as many problems as you can, listing things that might be done to ease each problem by kids, adults, schools, government, religious or civic groups, neighborhoods, sports teams, families, girls, boys, college students or professors, parent-teacher associations, or anyone else you might think of. When your list is done (or you simply want a break from listing solutions), sit down as a family and pick *one* approach to begin with. This will constitute your first family *tikun olam* pledge.

### The Family **Tikun Olam** *Pledge*

Take a new piece of paper and write down at the top, THE _____ FAMILY TIKUN OLAM PLEDGE. Underneath the heading, write a sentence that describes what you are pledging to do as a family first in order to address the problem you have selected. Then have each family member sign the pledge and agree on a timetable for implementing your plan. This can also be done as individual pledges, but the important thing is to pick something concrete that you are able to accomplish.

If you make this an ongoing family activity, you can involve children of any age in the process of making the world better. For example, you might decide that you want to help the environment suffer less from the greenhouse effect, and your first activity might be a pledge to plant a tree for every member of your family. Children of all ages can participate in the variety of activities necessary to fulfill this pledge, including choosing the kind of tree, finding a location, getting the necessary tools, the dirt, and the tree itself, and then helping with the actual planting. Your job as parent/ teacher is to join with your children in the activity while pointing out that what they are doing is fulfilling an important Jewish value, called *tikun olam*, repairing the world.

Another example might be to address some of the problems associated with the thousands of homeless children in our society. You might make your family *tikun olam* pledge to collect clothing from your neighbors and bring it to a shelter in your community that helps such families in need. This would allow all your children who can understand the concept to go into their own closets to find clothes or toys or blankets or such to share with the homeless children.

You might do the same with cans of food, or write letters to the local city officials asking them to help in organizing such a shelter if one doesn't already exist.

You could be like fourteen-year-old Trevor, who decided one day that his family would make sandwiches and other portable food, and drive their car around Philadelphia to deliver the food to the homeless who lived on the streets in his community. His personal act of *tikun olam* soon involved his entire family, neighborhood, city, and country when he was honored by then President Ronald Reagan for starting what became a community-wide program of feeding the homeless.

The possibilities are virtually endless. All it takes is for you to embrace *tikun olam* as a value worth teaching your children, and the willingness to participate with them in activities that bring it to life.

## Follow the Ten Commandments

If you ask most people who have grown up in the Western world to identify the foundation of their ethics, they will probably point to Most Important Jewish Idea #3: the Ten Commandments. That they exist as the cornerstone of Jewish and Western morality is, of course, much more widely remembered than the commandments themselves. Try to name all of them right now, and you will probably come up with only a few. Don't be upset, since when first asked, most people remember only "Don't kill" (which is actually "Don't murder"), "Don't commit adultery," and "Don't steal."

Yet it is these Ten Commandments (called Ten Statements in Hebrew: *Aseret ha-Dibrot*) that are the most often quoted foundation on which all subsequent ethics are based. That is why as our third in the top three most important Jewish ideas, I suggest "Follow the Ten Commandments."

The Ten Commandments have continued to inspire volumes of ethical dissertations, study, commentary, and exhortation throughout the thousands of years that they have influenced Western civilization. For your purposes in raising ethical Jewish children, they can serve as guidelines for a basic list of Jewish values.

Let's look at the actual Ten Commandments and remind ourselves of what they teach. The following is the list as presented in Exodus 20:2–14 (a slightly different version appears in Deuteronomy 5:6–18):

1. I am Adonai [a generic Hebrew name for God] your God, who brought you out of the land of Egypt, out of the house of bondage.

2. You shall have no other gods besides me.

3. You shall not use the name of Adonai your God in vain.

4. Remember the Sabbath day to make it holy.

5. Honor your father and mother.

6. You shall not murder.

7. You shall not commit adultery.

8. You shall not steal.

9. You shall not bear false witness against your neighbor.

10. You shall not covet your neighbor's house, your neighbor's wife . . . or anything that is your neighbor's.

Now that you have reviewed the commandments themselves, you may have a question about why the first one is included in such a list in the first place. It certainly doesn't seem to "command" us to do anything particular at all. In fact, many commentators throughout the centuries have asked exactly the same question, and arrived at different answers.

Most Jewish teachers have understood the first statement, "I am Adonai your God . . ." as an indirect command to believe in God. In fact, to my mind it is the quintessential Jewish statement of belief, because it doesn't actually say anything about belief at all! It forces us to *infer* the existence of a power greater than human beings by simply pointing to the single most powerful collective *experience* ever shared by the Jewish people, the Exodus from slavery in Egypt.

### God Is the Power That Inspires Freedom

Judaism is known for being a religion not of creed but of deed. It isn't faith that forms the basis of Jewish theology, it is facts. The fact is that we were slaves in Egypt, and at a particular moment in our history, we walked to freedom. The fact that we have celebrated freedom as the most fundamental "God-given" state of humanity is traced directly to our own personal Jewish experience of being enslaved.

The injunction to remember that we were slaves in Egypt happens to be the single most often repeated reminder in the Torah. Our slavery was without question the most powerful, most transforming, most ethically motivational experience in the entire four thousand years of Jewish history.

That is why the Ten Commandments begin with the simple reminder that what we call God is found in the power that transformed us from slaves to free people. The first commandment is really an exhortation to insist on freedom for everyone, to see freedom as the inalienable right of all people, and to recognize in that undying spark of freedom burning in the breast of every human being—no matter what religion, race, or country—the spark of godliness that can never be extinguished.

We are a people who base our understanding of God on direct experience, not on blind faith. Judaism doesn't demand of us that we suspend our understanding of how the universe actually works; rather, it points to the very mystery of the unfolding of nature, the intricacy of the human body, the inexplicable perfection of the stars and planets as they move in their orbits, the indomitable will of the human soul as concrete reflections of the divine presence in the world around us.

That is why the first commandment begins as it does. It establishes a kind of experiential credibility for the God who, according to Jewish tradition, is the power responsible for all the following commandments as well. The same transcendent power that inspired the Jewish people to break the bonds of their slavery and walk to freedom is the source of all universal ethics and morality, as reflected in the commandments that follow.

### Ethical Behavior as an Outgrowth of Humility

How do you teach this idea to your children? It starts with the willingness to point to the everyday miracles of life as evidence that the world is governed by powers and laws transcending human invention and design. To recognize that we are not the be-all and end-all of life, that there are forces in the universe much greater than us, but which we can use as sources of inspiration and awe—this is the first step to developing a spiritual approach to life.

It is equally important to help children grow up with an appropriate sense of their place in the universe, by reducing their natural tendency to unbridled arrogance and developing an understanding of the importance of humility. Ethical behavior is the result not only of training the everyday actions of your children by constant direction and feedback, but of a deeper sense of being connected to all life, responsible for the quality of the society in which we live, and humbled by the realization that we are but a tiny drop in the vast sea of the cosmos.

Take your children outside, away from the bright city lights on a clear night, and allow them to watch the stars. They can't help but be awed by the enormity, the magnificence of the universe in which we live and be reminded of their own smallness. Show them pictures of the earth taken from the moon. Ask them to point to the boundaries that divide one country from the next, and join in their "aha!" when they realize that there *aren't* such boundaries except as we human beings have artificially created them. That is a primary lesson in the oneness of humanity, pointing out that there is more that unites us than there is that divides us.

### God Is Not a Being Who Lives in the Sky

All these ideas come from the first commandment. They flow from the recognition that Judaism does not see God as some supernatural "Being" who lives in a heaven up in the sky and looks down upon the earth, choosing what will happen to each individual every moment. Rather, Judaism sees God as reflected in the actual experiences of human beings, the beauty of a flower, the inspiration of love, the strength of courage, the tenderness of compassion, and, as the first commandment reminds us, the act of personal freedom and liberation as well. Just look at all that has taken place throughout Eastern Europe, Africa, and the Soviet Union over the past few years and it will be obvious why this first commandment has retained its power and relevance throughout the centuries. The first commandment, then, is really "Learn that freedom is the inalienable divine right of every human being."

### The Second Commandment: Avoid Idolatry

The second commandment, "You shall have no other gods besides me," is a lesson in the importance of preventing idolatries of all kinds. In today's world in particular, our children are in danger of falling prey to the latest fads, the latest drugs, the latest thrills, the latest pop sensations, cult figures, and pseudoreligions.

For "idolatry" does not necessarily refer only to the worship of other religions or deities beyond that of the biblical Hebrews. For us, today, it refers to anything that assumes primary importance in our lives in a way that somehow diminishes the ethical values that Judaism teaches as being the foundation of our moral existence.

For example, when we become entrapped in addictions of all types, whether drugs, alcohol, food, gambling, or the host of other destructive compulsions to which our needy personalities might succumb, we have effectively elevated these addictions to the level of idols. *They* become the gods we worship, the motivations for our actions and thoughts, the driving force that runs our daily lives.

It is precisely against such idolatries that the second commandment is warning. If it were being written today, it would cry, "Stay clean, stay sober, stay healthy, take care of your body, your spirit, your mind, and fill your thoughts with positive, loving, nurturing, life-affirming ideas every day."

## The Idolatry of Excess

The 1980s became known as the decade of greed. The greed that fueled the scandals of Wall Street, Iran-Contra, failed savings and loans, and the rest was simply another form of idolatry that the second commandment warns against. Money must be a means to an end, not an end in itself. The Bible doesn't teach us that money is the root of all evil, only that the *pursuit* of money can lead us astray, blind us to the ultimate values that are truly important in our lives, and allow us to cause grief, pain, and suffering to those around us.

The idolatry that greed represents also finds expression in the self-indulgence that has become all too commonplace in modern society. Too many people act as if excess were the same as excellence, as if the more you consume the more you demonstrate your value as a human being.

The second commandment is a reminder that all such excesses, whether in the form of money, things, drugs, or celebrity worship, diminish our ability to live our lives according to the values that ennoble us, lift us up, inspire us, and bring the world closer to the kind of place we dream it can become.

You teach the lessons of the second commandment to your children first by supporting and participating in the programs that already exist in your community to combat drugs, alcohol, and the like in kids. But the primary way you teach these values to your children is by living them yourself. If you take drugs, drink alcohol every day, talk mostly about how much money you can make or are making, what clubs you can belong to, or act as if the acquisition of things is the ultimate goal of life, then you are passing those idolatries on to your children as well.

You can create projects with your children where the goal is to identify the important things of life. Have the members of your family write down the three things in your home most important to them, and compare notes. Ask what would happen if there were a fire and those things were destroyed. How crucial are they really in the day-to-day lives of your family? If you never had them again, how would it affect you?

Now write down (or share verbally with kids who are too young to write comfortably) the three most important things in your life that aren't things (such as people, or relationships, or feelings, or qualities or personality traits or abilities). Imagine how different your lives would be if *these* were missing, and it becomes obvious immediately where your true values lie. Even small children will understand that it is more important to have the love of parents and siblings and the freedom to live life as they choose than to have the latest Nintendo game or doll that turns into a flying machine.

### The Third Commandment: Integrity

The third commandment is usually mistranslated and misunderstood to mean that one shouldn't swear (as in goddamn) or say the word *God* when you don't really mean it in a religious sense. The real meaning of "You shall not use the name of Adonai your God in vain" refers to an ancient practice of calling upon one's ultimate authority (in this case, God) when making a vow or a pledge. It is similar to the practice today of being sworn in in a court room by raising your right hand and promising ("so help me God") to tell the truth in what you are about to say.

Promising to tell the truth, and convincing others that it really *is* the truth by using God as a kind of spiritual collateral, when in fact you are lying degrades the image of God in the eyes of the world.

The lesson to be learned here is how important it is to be someone others can count on. Integrity is one of the most crucial attributes any human being can have. The Talmud teaches that of all the attributes a human being can have, the most important is "a good name." A good name means that people can trust you, that your yes is a yes, and your no is a no. It means that when you say you will do something, others can believe that it will happen.

That is why included in one of the Ten Commandments is this warning not to use the name of God frivolously in making promises. In this sense, *God* is used to represent the highest and most significant values you embrace. If you are willing to denigrate even the most precious values in your life by using them to lie to others, then you are obviously not worthy of anyone's trust ever.

You teach your children integrity by insisting that they keep their word. As I will repeat throughout this book, children learn what they live, primarily from the examples your life provides. You carry the heaviest responsibility for demonstrating to your children what integrity means. They must experience it firsthand by watching you, learning from how you act, seeing how you treat others, and realizing that you and your word can be counted on. That is the single most important way you teach integrity to another—by demonstrating it yourself.

Also be aware of the inevitable times when your children (and you) are let down by others who fall short of keeping their word. Point out how disappointed you are, how upsetting it is to live in a world in which you can't count on people to do what they say, and how much you respect and admire those people in your life who do have integrity.

You will have ample opportunities to demonstrate to your children the difference between integrity and its absence. Praise them every time they follow through on a promise, whether it's to go to bed at a particular time, return in time for dinner, clean up their room, do the dishes, finish their homework before watching television, or whatever. The specific deed makes no difference at all. The point is that you show you're proud of them every time they demonstrate integrity and trustworthiness. It is up to you to reinforce again and again how singularly important this quality is to you, and how crucial it is to making the world a better place.

### The Fourth Commandment: Make Life Holy

The fourth commandment is a reminder that we have the power to make life holy, special, and extraordinary. Judaism gave a beautiful gift to the world when it introduced the idea of the Sabbath. To teach that once every seven days we are to refrain from work so that we can bring holiness into our lives was a spiritual boon the rest of the world still needs badly.

The point isn't whether you celebrate Shabbat in a traditional Jewish fashion (as I mentioned in Chapter 1), it is whether you create a balance in your life between work and play, home and office, creativity and regeneration. The fourth commandment can be used as a tool to teach your children about the importance of taking control of that which is in their power, and not allowing outside forces to dictate the quality of their lives.

Shabbat can be a metaphor for achieving mastery over our lives, creating time to contemplate who we are, where we are going, what our goals are in life, and the kind of people we wish to become. It is a symbol of consciousness, for it reminds us that, unlike animals, who can act only in accordance with preordained instincts, we human beings have the power to write our own life stories, to chart our own courses, to make conscious choices concerning just about everything that is important in our lives.

The best way to teach these values to your children is to guide them in making intelligent choices at the different stages of their lives. Begin when they are young by giving them alternatives to choose from, praising them whenever they make positive, constructive choices.

As they get older, help them by creating a structure that allows for both work and play, school and extracurricular activities, while pointing out the value of having this balance in their lives. It is also important for them to realize that they have the ability to make life holy, special, or sacred. Setting aside time to view a spectacular sunset, giving of themselves to help another by tutoring, extending a hand when needed to lighten another's load—these are examples of what holiness is all about.

In a sense, successful parenting is a function of what I call "mitzvah framing." A mitzvah in traditional Jewish language is the equivalent of a commandment. As I use it, it represents any ethical act or religious obligation— it is "doing the right thing" in a given circumstance, and can inevitably be linked to one of these important Jewish ethical values we are discussing.

Mitzvah framing means taking the activities, experiences, and opportunities you find in your life and the lives of your children and placing an ethical concept, idea, or commandment around them like a frame. It means pausing when you see your child help another to *say* to your child, "I'm proud of you when you do a mitzvah like that." "I love seeing you demonstrating the mitzvah of loving your neighbor as yourself," or "following the Golden Rule," or "making the world a better place for everyone."

### The Fifth Commandment: Honoring Parents

The fifth commandment, "Honor your father and your mother," is an essential foundation on which the very stability of our society rests. If arises from the recognition that for society to flourish and allow for an orderly transition from one generation to the next, it is crucial to instill in the young a sense of respect for those who have come before.

In particular, Judaism holds up the family unit as *the* crucial building block of all society. The importance of the family as the center of Jewish life is most clearly seen in the fact that almost all Jewish holidays and festivals are celebrated with the family in the home. It is in the family that values, ethics, rituals, customs, and culture are most powerfully taught. It is in the family that respect for others and the recognition of the worth and dignity of all people are instilled in your children.

The family setting provides perhaps the most perfect opportunity for framing the positive actions of your children in terms of specific Jewish ethics. As with all ethical lessons, the most effective way to teach this commandment to your children is to model it in your own behavior. For example, when you send a birthday or anniversary card to your own parents, you can tell your children that it is a simple way to act out the fifth commandment in your own life.

Honoring your own parents obviously can take many forms. Sending cards or letters, making sure your children hear you call your parents to see how they are doing, expressing your concern and love for them at the dinner table when your children are present, all establish a model of how you live the fifth commandment every day.

Furthermore, just as taking care of your own parents communicates the importance of the fifth commandment to your children, so too anytime your children are polite or thoughtful or respectful of you is an appropriate time to commend them for fulfilling this traditional Jewish mitzvah.

### The Sixth Commandment: Don't Murder

The sixth commandment, "You shall not murder," is often mistranslated as "You shall not kill." Obviously, murder is not the same as killing. In fact, Jewish tradition specifically condones killing in self-defense, and teaches that if someone pursues you with the intent to kill, you are commanded to kill that person first.

In any event, when it comes to child rearing, the sixth commandment is perhaps best understood as reflecting the fundamental Jewish belief in the sanctity of life. Murder is morally wrong, because all human life is sacred. Your job as parent is to teach your child to value every human being as if that person carried a spark of the divine within.

The sixth commandment can be a challenge to raise your children to look for the good in other people. Murder and war ultimately come about because one human being is able to see another as not only less valuable but somehow less human than he or she. That is why the "enemy" is always spoken of in negative, slang language designed to rob them of their humanity and distance them emotionally from us. "Kraut," "Jap,"

"Gook" are words that make human beings sound not human at all, and therefore make them easier to kill.

You can use the sixth commandment as a reminder that *all* people share the same hopes and dreams, frustrations and desires, no matter what their color, country of origin, or language. Teach your children not only to respect people who are different but to see what can be learned from them. Stop them from using derogatory slang terms for other ethnic groups. Don't laugh at, tell, or permit others to tell derogatory ethnic jokes in your presence. In this way you teach the dignity of all people, the sanctity of all human life, and ultimately why the sixth commandment forbids us to murder other human beings, no matter who they might be.

### The Seventh Commandment: Don't Commit Adultery

"You shall not commit adultery," the seventh commandment, is naturally assumed to be a topic for adults only. The truth, however, is that what underlies this commandment is the value of family stability, the value that Judaism places on the institution of marriage, and ultimately the importance of raising children who are able to commit to loving, nurturing, lasting relationships.

You prepare your children for this commandment when they are small, by teaching integrity, honesty, and trust. When you reward them for being honest (even if it's to tell you they did something they weren't supposed to), when you give praise each time you trust them and they come through for you, it builds the positive self-esteem so necessary for integrity and trustworthiness later in life.

The seventh commandment is necessary because we live in a world where too many people are raised in families in which there is precious little trust to begin with. Children need boundaries and a structure they can count on. They need mothers and fathers who give them unconditional love, who encourage them with praise and positive feedback, who build a world around them that is stable, secure, and safe. When this is done, they have a much better chance of being trustworthy and reliable when they grow up and are functioning in relationships as adults.

### The Eighth Commandment: Don't Steal

Related to this need for developing positive self-esteem is the eighth commandment, "You shall not steal." In many cases, stealing is a reflection of an inner neediness that stems from a childhood filled with insecurity, tension, anxiety, and fear. Stealing is a negative way of exercising control over one's environment, by laying claim to things that otherwise are under the control of another.

The eighth commandment can serve as a teaching tool for emphasizing respect for others in an otherwise "me-first" world. You teach your children not to steal in different ways, depending on their age level. For the younger child, a straightforward quid pro quo is all they can understand: You don't steal because you don't want others to steal from you.

As kids get older, you can teach them the primary reason for not stealing is that we are responsible for creating the society we live in. We want to live in a world where we can trust others, and others can trust us. We want to live in a world of integrity, fairness, justice, dignity, and compassion. To do so requires that we act in such a way as to bring the world closer to that model each day. "You shall not steal" is one of the rules necessary for such a world to exist, both now and in the future.

### The Ninth Commandment: Don't Lie

The ninth commandment is "You shall not bear false witness against your neighbor." It is directly related to the two preceding commandments in that at root its primary purpose is to reinforce the central importance of integrity in all relationships.

All social issues concern interpersonal relationships, whether between a person and his or her neighbor, a husband and wife, or parents and children. Contained in the simple, straightforward messages of the Ten Commandments are the fundamental principles necessary to establish order, security, trust, and human dignity.

"Bearing false witness" against another is, in the language of children, *lying*. In fact, if you rephrase the ninth commandment as "Don't lie," it is immediately clear how relevant this particular mitzvah is to the lives of children.

Practically every child in the world lies at one time or another. It might be as relatively harmless as disclaiming responsibility for something they did, denying they broke one of the family behavior rules, claiming to have finished their homework when they haven't or that they didn't eat the last piece of cake in the refrigerator.

Lying for children is often a test of the adult world's tolerance of unacceptable behavior. It is one of the ways kids search for boundaries and ask (albeit unconsciously) for adult intervention. Part of your job as a parent is to be clear about the importance of truth and honesty with your children, and to insist on it at every opportunity.

There are countless examples of the consequences of lying, particularly about other people. Lives and reputations have been ruined needlessly by unfounded slander, families and marriages torn apart by vicious rumors. Every child can provide his own personal recollections of occasions when someone said something about him that wasn't true.

Ask your children to recall such a time. How did they feel? How did they feel about the other person? What did they want to do about it? What could they do (if anything) to counteract what other people thought about them as a result of the untrue accusation? You might role-play with your children an example of the damage that results when gossip is spread about another person, and ask them to devise rules for behavior that might remind people how painful and harmful such experiences can be.

### Slander Is Close to Murder

Judaism even has a special term in Hebrew for this behavior: *lashon ha-ra*, which literally means "a bad tongue." We actually have a similar expression in English. When someone speaks badly of another person, we say she is "bad-mouthing" that person. The rabbis of Jewish tradition were so concerned about the power people have to hurt one another with words that they compared the damage done to another human being through a "bad tongue" (gossip and slander) to murder, saying that destroying another person's good name has the potential to destroy her livelihood and ultimately her very life.

You might share with your children the following story from Jewish tradition. A man in a small town is angry at someone, and so goes around spreading lies about him to his friends and acquaintances. After a while his anger cools, and he begins to feel bad about all the nasty things he had been saying, so he goes to the local rabbi seeking forgiveness. The rabbi tells him to cut open a pillow and walk around town tossing the feathers in the air one at a time until the pillow is empty.

He finds this a rather strange suggestion, but because he is feeling guilty about his actions, he does what the rabbi asks. After he has finished and returns to the rabbi for more instructions, the rabbi tells him, "Now go back and pick up all the feathers and put them back into the pillow."

"But Rabbi," the man exclaims, "that is impossible. By now the wind has scattered the feathers so far I could never retrieve them."

"Ahh," says the rabbi. "It is exactly the same with your words. *They* will be as impossible to retrieve as the feathers. Once they leave your mouth, you can never control how far they may travel or what damage they may do."

It undermines the very fabric of our society when people perjure themselves and innocent people are found guilty of crimes they never committed. So, too, it destroys our ability to have faith in the people to whom we entrust the governing of our society when they take bribes and manipulate the legal and legislative system for personal gain, regardless of the impact on the lives of others. These are all instances in which someone has ignored the ninth commandment. Unfortunately, examples with which to teach your children can be found practically every day in your local newspaper.

### The Tenth Commandment: Appreciate What You Have

The single most important key to satisfaction in life is hidden in the commandment not to covet our neighbor's property. To covet means to desire something that belongs to someone else. To properly understand the implications of this commandment is to discover what Judaism teaches about achieving fulfillment, satisfaction, and joy in life.

At root, the tenth commandment really has nothing to do with other people at all. It revolves around the simple idea that one of the greatest sources of unhappiness in life is the feeling that you never have enough. The fact is, no matter how much of anything you have, you could always have more: more money, more things, more friends, more houses, more cars, more vacation, more love.

### Who Is Rich?

The rabbis of the Talmud recognized that being happy in life has very little to do with how much money you make, the size of your home, or the toys that you accumulate. They ask the rhetorical question, "Who is rich?" and reply "One who is happy with what he or she has." Frustration, anxiety, anger, jealousy, unhappiness are all a result of never being satisfied with our lot in life. Those who experience true joy in living are the ones who celebrate the blessings and gifts they *do* have, rather than grumble over the things they don't.

I believe the single best piece of advice I have ever given my daughter is to be happy about what she has rather than sad about what she doesn't have. The American obsession called "keeping up with the Joneses" has probably sowed more seeds of discontent than all the economic recessions and depressions in history.

Teaching your children to value and appreciate life as they live it, to cultivate the ability to recognize the blessings and miracles that fill their lives each day, is one of the most important gifts you will ever give them.

An easy way of getting this lesson across (and a good thing to do while riding in the car on a trip) is to have everyone in the family call out the things they have that they love the most. What are their favorite things in their rooms, at school, or at work? Who are their favorite friends and relatives? Where are their favorite places to go or things to see and do? How about the abilities, skills, and personality traits they are most proud of?

After listing all these blessings that fill their lives, talk about all the children in the world who have never had these opportunities, don't have these abilities, and probably will never experience the things your children are able to. The idea isn't to feel guilty for what you have and others don't, it's to train yourself and your children to recognize the gifts and wonders that fill your lives each day.

The tenth commandment is a subtle program for fulfillment. Being able to appreciate whatever you have in life, whatever age you are, whatever stage of growth, learning, and development you are experiencing at the moment, is *the* biggest key to satisfaction and happiness. Furthermore, the most wonderful part of it all is that this happiness is *totally* in your control, and the control of your children, for it depends on only one thing: your attitude.

## The Power of Attitude

*Attitude* is probably the single most powerful word in the entire English language. *Attitude* is responsible for the very quality of your life and the lives of your children. It certainly isn't the specific experiences or circumstances of life that determine your happiness, but rather the attitude you bring to these experiences.

"You shall not covet" is a reminder that all your happiness can come from within. Once your basic needs for food, shelter, and love are met, the rest is determined by your attitude about life. Teaching your children to be happy with who they are, with what they have, with their own particular and unique talents and abilities, strengths and weaknesses, is giving them the gift of happiness in life.

Obviously, there are hundreds of other ethical ideas, values, and lessons you will want to share with your children. This chapter was designed to give you a start in the right direction, by sharing some of the major ethical ideas that Judaism has brought to the world: "Love your neighbor as yourself," "We are partners in completing the work of creation," and "Follow the Ten Commandments."

Next we turn to some of the most important holidays of the Jewish year, to see how they, too, teach important values to your children.

# Three

# Celebrating Holidays and the Values They Teach

*Every inheritance of the Jewish people,
every teaching of their secular history and
religious experience, draws them powerfully
to the side of charity, liberty and progress.*
                              *Calvin Coolidge*

Most Jews experience Judaism primarily through the celebration of holidays. Even those who don't see themselves as religious will usually be found lighting candles on Hanukah or having a Seder on Passover. For such Jews, the marking off of these moments during the year as special Jewish times serves as a primary reinforcer of their Jewish identity. These holidays not only link them emotionally with Jewish history (since the holidays themselves recall specific historical events of the Jewish past), they connect them with Jews throughout the world who are celebrating these same holidays at the same time.

Since Judaism is a culture of actions rather than beliefs, its most important values come to life through the holiday customs of the Jewish year. They provide a concrete, hands-on approach to expressing one's Jewish identity, for the celebrations center around simple family rituals that can be carried out by adults and children in the home, regardless of the level of their Jewish background.

In many ways, creating your own religious lifestyle means integrating the key holidays of the Jewish year into the life of your family. This chapter will introduce you to those holidays that are celebrated by the largest number of Jews (Hanukah, Passover, Shabbat) and show how you can use them to teach key values to your children. You will also discover the secret to what I call "The Ten-Minute Holiday."

The Ten-Minute Holiday makes it easy for you and your family to experiment with new ways of celebrating holidays and trying out new Jewish customs each year. The key is to find ways of marking these special days each year that encourage participation, are easy to understand, and bring satisfaction and pleasure to everyone.

## Hanukah: The First Fight
## for Religious Freedom

Hanukah is undoubtedly the best known of all Jewish holidays. It owes this fame, in no small part, to its annual proximity to Christmas. Originally a relatively minor holiday in Jewish tradition, Hanukah has grown in importance during this century as Jews have felt a need to compete with the glamour and attraction created by the commercialization and heavy promotion of Christmas.

The two holidays have virtually nothing in common, except that they both use the symbolism of light. The Christmas trees and decorations that adorn Christian houses during this season are aglow with multicolored lights. And Hanukah is called "The Festival of Lights." But it is a light of a different nature, a light that represents a radically different reality from that of Christmas.

For Christianity, Christmas marks the moment when God adopted human form (called "Jesus") in order to "come down" from heaven and provide people with the means of solving the problems they had created on earth. The lights of Christmas represent the divine light that, according to Christianity, Jesus brought into the world by his birth, and the promise of the divine light of grace symbolized by his voluntary death.

For the Jewish people, the lights of Hanukah symbolize the light of religious freedom. The story of Hanukah is the story of the first recorded struggle for religious freedom, and after the victory was won, light itself became an important part of the story.

In the year 167 B.C.E. ("before the common era," the preferred Jewish equivalent of B.C., which Christians use to mean "before Christ") the Syrian emperor Antiochus decided to unify his kingdom by insisting that all people (including the Jews) adopt the same religion—the worship of Zeus. He therefore forbade circumcision and the teaching or practice of Judaism upon pain of death, and ordered the Jews to abandon the Torah and publicly embrace paganism, the sacrifice of pigs, and bowing down to an idol of Zeus.

Many Jews were, indeed, put to death, but a Jew named Mattathias, along with his five sons, refused to accept this repressive policy of Jewish self-destruction, and took to the hills in revolt. They inspired others to join them in a struggle which lasted for three years. Though the Jews were vastly outnumbered by the Syrian army, when the torch of leadership passed upon the death of Mattathias to his son Judah the Maccabee ("the hammer" in Hebrew), Judah led a brilliant campaign of guerrilla warfare which retook the road to Jerusalem and ultimately climaxed in the routing of the Syrian army and the liberation of Jerusalem and its sacred temple.

Hanukah (which literally means "dedication") is the celebration of the victory of the Maccabees (as the entire rebel army came to be called) over the Syrian army, and the rededication of the temple in Jerusalem to its rightful place as the center of Jewish worship.

According to the legend that grew up around this remarkable victory, when the Maccabees entered the temple for the rededication, they could find only a small jar of oil with which to light the temple menorah (candelabrum), which should have lasted just one day. Miraculously, it lasted eight days, which allowed them to prepare enough ritually pure oil to complete the rededication ceremony and keep the sacred menorah lit continuously.

Jewish tradition has taught that in commemoration
of this miracle of the lights, we celebrate Hanukah for
eight days. Many modern scholars argue that this story
was really fabricated long after the victory of the Maccabees to emphasize God's role in our deliverance
from the plan of evil Antiochus, and to play down the
importance of militarism and success by might of
arms. Regardless of the literal truth of the legend of
the oil that burned for eight days, the true miracle
we celebrate on Hanukah is the miracle of religious
freedom.

### Teaching Values Through
### the Celebration of Hanukah

Hanukah is an annual reminder that religious freedom
is truly a precious gift. It can help keep us aware that
we must be ever vigilant to protect the rights of all peoples; to ensure that everyone, regardless of religious belief, continues to have the right to practice and celebrate
as he or she chooses, free from the tyranny of coercion.

Hanukah provides a wonderful opportunity to teach
several vital values to your children. Obviously, the primary value is the importance of religious freedom. You
teach this first by telling the story of Hanukah itself, the
drama of brave Mattathias, Judah, and his brothers as
they fought against overwhelming odds to defeat the
bigger, more powerful Syrian army. If it weren't for
the Maccabees and the victory of Hanukah, none of us
would be Jews today; our entire religious civilization
would have come to a tragic end.

Second, Hanukah raises one of those crucial questions that all of us are confronted with during our lives,
namely, "What is worth fighting for?" The celebration
of Hanukah can provide the opportunity to examine

the implications of this profound question with your adolescent or older children.

Let me offer a few specific suggestions as to how these values can be addressed and communicated. The easiest way to approach the lessons of Hanukah is through the simple Hanukah family rituals. It is essentially a family holiday, and its celebration takes place in your own home with your family and friends.

As you may know already, the primary way we celebrate Hanukah is by lighting lights each night for eight nights. Most people use a Hanukah menorah (called *Hanukiya* in Hebrew) with colored candles, but some people create their own or use oil lamps that burn olive oil. Creating your own Hanukah menorah is a wonderful family project, for it gives you the opportunity to express your own family's thoughts on freedom as you work together. Resources for learning how to do Jewish family crafts projects can be found in Chapter 7.

The traditional way of lighting the menorah is to light one candle on the first night (plus the *shamash*, or "helper" candle), and add an additional candle each night until the entire menorah is filled on the last night. Some families have a separate menorah for each member of the family, others take turns lighting the lights of a single menorah each night. Whatever way works best for your family is fine.

A special ceremony accompanies the lighting. Customarily, the candles are placed in the menorah from right to left and lit from left to right—thus the candle that signifies the night of Hanukah you are celebrating is lit first. After the candles are placed, the shamash is lit first, and it is then used to light the other candles.

The custom of using a helper candle came about because, according to Jewish law, the Hanukah candles were not to be used for any purpose other than publicizing the miracle of Hanukah itself. Therefore, in case someone would accidentally use the menorah to see or read with, he or she could say that it was really the shamash and not the Hanukah lights being used. Though most people know nothing about these origins of the shamash, its use has continued as an expected part of the ritual of the lights of Hanukah.

Now to the ritual itself. Either before or while lighting the candles, the following two blessings are traditionally recited (the Hebrew can be found in the Glossary of Hebrew Blessings at the end of the book):

> Blessed are you our God, divine power of the universe, who makes our lives special through commandments, and commands us to kindle the Hanukah lights.

> Blessed are you our God, divine power of the universe, who performed miracles for our ancestors in days of old at this season.

On the first night of Hanukah only, the blessing known as the *sheheheyanu* prayer is recited. It is used to mark the beginning of every holiday or special time, and many Jews recite it whenever they do something special for the first time. It also happens to be my daughter Gable's favorite prayer, and she likes to use it when we do *anything* for the first time as a family.

The *sheheheyanu* gives thanks for the fact that we have lived to be able to celebrate this occasion, and goes like this:

> Blessed are you our God, divine power of the universe, who has kept us in life, sustained us and allowed us to reach this special moment together.

As I mentioned, Jewish tradition teaches that the menorah candles are lit in order to make known and publicize the miracle of Hanukah. In olden days the menorah was lighted outside, in front of the house by the street, so that passersby would see the lights and be reminded of the miracle of Jewish survival and the fight for religious freedom. Today Jews traditionally place the menorah in a window (unless there are curtains which make it dangerous), to serve both as a sign of the miracle of Hanukah and a symbol of pride in being Jewish and having holidays to celebrate.

You might ask each family member as the menorah is lit to name one freedom he or she thinks is important today. Each night you can add another freedom to the list, which might be written on a large piece of colored paper and used as part of the Hanukah decorations in your home. This acts as an additional reminder of the freedoms we cherish, and reinforces the lessons of the holiday each time the list is read.

Another family activity is to find physical symbols of our freedoms and place them in a conspicuous spot in the living room or wherever Hanukah is celebrated. These can be objects you make, pictures cut out of magazines, or items of your own such as a book, flag, model of the Statue of Liberty, photograph, or anything else that represents a freedom worth celebrating.

Celebrating Hanukah has become the most joyous family time of the Jewish year. It is a time to exchange presents (many families give one present each night for eight nights), a time to sing songs about Hanukah and freedom, to play games and eat special Hanukah foods. Many families invite others to their home to join in their celebration, and the proximity of Christmas provides a wonderful opportunity for Jews and non-Jews to share each other's holidays and learn about each other's customs.

The most famous Hanukah game is called dreidel. It uses a special four-sided spinning top, with a different Hebrew letter which together stand for the phrase, "A great miracle happened there" (in Israel one letter is changed and the phrase is "A great miracle happened here"). The top is spun and, depending on which letter is showing, the spinner either wins the pot (which is usually special Hanukah candy in the form of gold-foil-covered chocolate coins), takes half, gets nothing, or has to put in more.

Two special foods that are associated with Hanukah are potato pancakes (called *latkes* in Yiddish) and jelly doughnuts (called *sufganiyot* in Hebrew). Both became Hanukah foods because they are fried in oil, which is a reminder of the jar of oil that lasted eight days and allowed the rededication of the temple in Jerusalem to take place after the Maccabee victory.

You can celebrate Hanukah any way you wish. The ideal is to be creative and add something new and different of your own design each year. Some of my fondest childhood memories are of my sisters and me making our own Hanukah decorations with my parents. One year we each drew pictures of our favorite freedoms on large paper and hung them around the house. Another year we created a mural that depicted important moments in Jewish history, and moments in history that represented significant freedoms we are blessed with.

You can do the same on a simpler (or, for that matter, more ambitious) scale in your own family. Pick one thing to do each year, and add it to your celebration repertoire. When your children are young, have them help you make potato pancakes or jelly doughnuts (of course, driving to the doughnut shop is quicker!), or have them draw their own pictures of Judah Maccabee, or fighting for freedom, or the Hanukah menorah, or a jar of oil, or any other Hanukah scene, and place these as decorations around the room.

As they get older they can participate more fully in the identification of values and freedoms worth fighting for. These, too, can become symbols of the holidays used to decorate your home. Making the home as festive and beautiful as possible is part of the traditional way Jews celebrate every holiday. There is an ancient Jewish concept, *hiddur mitzvah* (the "beauty of the command-ment"), which refers to the beauty we can create to sur-round any Jewish custom, holiday, or tradition. Use your imagination, don't be intimidated by a lack of knowledge or Jewish experience, and you will discover that Hanukah can be one of the most joyous and loving family experiences of the year.

## Passover: Liberation and Renewal

According to most surveys, the holiday celebrated by more Jews than any other each year is Passover. Pass-over holds a power and fascination for young and old alike. It is a special time when families gather to share a festive meal in which they eat strange, exotic foods, drink four cups of wine, and tell the story of how our ancestors were liberated from slavery in Egypt.

Rich with rituals and symbols, songs and stories, all designed to remind us that for the Jewish people, free-dom is the most important of all human values, Pass-over is the quintessential home holiday. Its celebration centers around the family dinner table, where an elaborate dinner party called a Seder (meaning "order" in Hebrew) takes place.

The meal is called a Seder because there is a definite order to the various rituals, foods, and stories that are told. Participants follow a guidebook called a Haggadah ("telling" in Hebrew), which gives step-by-step instructions regarding which foods to eat in what order and their meanings, which stories to tell, when to drink the wine, and even which songs to sing.

Passover's universal themes of liberation from all forms of bondage, freedom from hunger and want, and the rebirth and renewal of spring touch the hearts of everyone. It is a holiday that is most fully appreciated when shared with others, whether the extended family or friends. In fact, the beginning of the Seder contains a phrase in Aramaic (the language popular around the time of Jesus), which calls out, "Let all who are hungry come and eat. Let all who are in need come and share the Passover with us."

It is easy to see why Passover has always served as a concrete lesson in human responsibility and interrelatedness. One cannot share a Seder meal without realizing the importance of all people being freed from the oppression of hunger and poverty, homelessness and want. At every turn, the rituals teach us that Judaism believes freedom and justice to be the natural, God-given state human beings were meant to enjoy.

In a sense, teaching your children the lessons of Passover is the easiest task of all. To do so, all you need is to have them participate in the Seder itself, sharing the unusual Passover foods and hearing the stories of slavery and freedom. The holiday is a self-contained educational experience, which in each generation has taught us its crucial and powerful lessons.

The name "Passover" comes from the biblical story (dramatized in the famous movie *The Ten Commandments*) in which death passes over the houses of the Israelite slaves during the tenth and final plague. Although Pharaoh had decreed that all Israelite baby boys were to be thrown into the Nile and drowned, this tenth plague caused the death of all firstborn Egyptians instead. It was only then that Pharaoh's spirit was broken and he allowed the Israelites to go free.

Passover is the celebration of this freedom after four hundred years of slavery in Egypt. In it we retell the story of our slavery and liberation (with the help of Moses and his brother Aaron and sister Miriam), and pledge to do whatever we can to see that all people are free as well.

One of the most fascinating aspects of Jewish civilization is that we celebrate and glorify the slavery of our ancestors. Most people long to forget the poverty and degradation of their past, obscuring it from memory and glorifying instead the successes and heights to which they and their family have risen. The Jewish people, on the other hand, use the slavery of their past as a constant object lesson for the present and future. In fact, Jewish tradition goes so far as to command every Jew to recall the slavery of our past as a *personal* experience. The Haggadah from which we read on the night of the Passover Seder states, "In every generation each person is obligated to feel as if he or she personally went forth from the slavery of Egypt."

This personal experience of slavery is our collective way of ensuring that we never become too complacent; that we never sit back and think that freeing the world from slavery, poverty, and injustice is someone else's responsibility. Passover reminds us year in and year out that because we know what it is like to be slaves, we must help all others who are enslaved. Because we know what it is like to be a stranger in a foreign land, we must extend ourselves to help strangers in our own land as well.

Each year as we celebrate Passover, we have another opportunity to teach these lessons to our children. If you have never celebrated Passover before, you will find simple directions and explanations in most Passover Haggadahs that you can buy in a bookstore. Local synagogues often have workshops and one-time seminars designed for those who want to learn how to run their own Seder. In addition, you will find additional resources listed at the end of the book in Chapter 7.

### The Symbols of the Seder

Although the Bible declares that Passover is to be celebrated as a seven-day festival (it is celebrated by Orthodox and Conservative Jews outside of Israel for eight days), the primary observance takes place the first night at the Seder meal. Many Jews also have a Seder on the second night either in their homes or at their synagogues. The second-night Seder is often made different in tone and character from the first by focusing on a particular theme, like freedom for Soviet Jews, Jews and others persecuted in foreign lands, ecology and the liberation of the earth from human destruction, women's liberation, interfaith Seders, and the like.

The symbols of Passover are found on the ceremonial Seder plate that usually sits in front of the leader:

- *Roasted shankbone* symbolizes the Passover offering brought to the temple in Jerusalem in ancient times (when animal sacrifices were a normal part of religious ceremonies). It also reminds us of the biblical phrase that God redeemed us from slavery "with an outstretched arm." Furthermore, it is a reminder that on the actual night of liberation from Egypt, the Israelite slaves had enough faith in the power of freedom to slaughter lambs, which were a symbol of Egyptian gods, and put the blood on their doors in the very faces of their Egyptian masters.

* *Maror (bitter herbs)*—usually grated horseradish root or romaine lettuce—to symbolize the bitterness of slavery.

* *Karpas (parsley)*, or any green herb or vegetable, represents spring, renewal, rebirth, and hope for the future. In addition, during the Seder the parsley is dipped in salt water (a symbol of the tears of slavery) to remind us that despair (tears) must always be mixed with hope. It is also a reminder of how our ancestors used a leafy vegetable as a brush to smear the blood of the lambs on their doorposts on the night of their liberation.

* A *roasted egg* symbolizes the continuing cycles of life (since it is round); it also serves as a reminder of the special holiday offering brought to the temple in Jerusalem in ancient times. Some people see it as a symbol of the Jewish people's will to survive. Just as an egg becomes harder and harder as you boil it in hot water, so too the Jewish people continue to emerge from the heat of persecution and oppression stronger and more resilient than ever.

* *Haroset (mixture of nuts, apples, wine, and cinnamon)* serves as a symbol of the mortar that the Israelites

used during their slavery to make bricks to build cities for Pharaoh.

The best known of all the symbolic foods of Passover is matzah. Matzah is simply unleavened bread that is used both during the Seder meal and throughout the week of Passover, since the primary commandment of the holiday is to avoid eating anything that is leavened (called hametz in Hebrew).

In addition to the Seder plate with the symbolic foods listed above, three ceremonial pieces of matzah are placed in the center of the table (or in front of the leader). These represent the two traditional loaves of bread that were a part of every holiday (to remind us that, according to the Bible, God provided a double portion of food for our ancestors during their forty years of wandering in the desert each Sabbath, so they wouldn't have to work to gather food), plus an extra matzah to symbolize Passover itself. Today, many people set out a fourth matzah, called "the Matzah of Hope," to remind us of those many Jews in foreign lands who are still not free to live and celebrate as they choose.

Matzah is first mentioned in the Bible in the book of Exodus (12:34–39), where we learn that the Israelites left Egypt in such a hurry (wouldn't you if you were a slave going free?) that they simply slapped their dough on their backs and it baked in the hot desert sun without rising. Thus we eat matzah on Passover to remind us of our rush to freedom.

Matzah is also called the "bread of affliction," since slaves eat only the simplest of foods, such as bread made with just flour and water like matzah. Therefore, every time we eat matzah it recalls both our slavery *and* our freedom, and thus it is the perfect ritual symbol for the entire Passover season.

Toward the beginning of the Seder, the middle matzah (of the ceremonial three) is broken, and half (called the afikomen) is hidden away by the leader (to be stolen, they hope, by the children) for use at the end of the meal. This is often a highlight for the children, who, upon discovering its hiding place, can bargain with the leader for prizes, money, candy, or gifts before returning it to him or her, since the Seder is not supposed to end without it.

### The Four Questions

One of the most important elements of the Seder itself is the asking of questions. The Seder is *designed* to provoke questions, especially from children, who sit and wonder about the unusual foods, the elaborate Seder table, and all the excitement of the evening. Almost everything is designed to stimulate questions, answers, and discussions. In fact, Jewish tradition says that the longer you talk about the experience of being slaves and going free from Egypt, the more praiseworthy you are!

The most famous of all questions during the Seder are called "The Four Questions." They are traditionally asked by the youngest child who is able, but really, of course, anyone can ask them. Their purpose is to bring to our attention some of the unusual elements of the evening, and invite the leader (or anyone else who wants to join in) to retell the story of the Exodus from Egypt. The four questions are:

Why is this night different from all other nights?

1. On all other nights we eat leavened or unleavened bread; tonight why do we eat only unleavened?

2. On all other nights we eat all kinds of vegetables; tonight why do we eat only bitter herbs?

3. On all other nights we are not required to dip at our meal; tonight why do we dip two times (parsley in salt water, and bitter herbs in haroset)?

4. On all other nights we eat either seated upright or reclining; tonight why do we all recline? (We are told to recline since in ancient times it was a sign of a free person. Usually the leader of the Seder has a pillow to symbolize reclining.)

The remainder of the Seder is really a response to these four questions. They form the framework around which the answers are given, and the stories that unfold carry with them the essence of the lessons contained in the festival of Passover itself.

### Opening the Door for Elijah

One of the best-remembered and best-loved moments in the Passover Seder takes place when someone (usually a child) is asked to open the door for Elijah, the biblical prophet who, according to tradition, will return to announce the coming of the Messiah or messianic age, which will bring freedom, peace, justice, and redemption to the entire world.

There is always an aura of excitement when the door is opened for Elijah, and it creates a kind of mystical moment when all our hopes for the future of the world are drawn together in the symbol of this ancient prophet. We set out a special glass of wine (called the Cup of Elijah) that sits in the center of our table untouched throughout the Seder, waiting for Elijah to enter and drink.

Since Passover is a holiday that celebrates the liberation of our past and the freedoms we dream of for the future, Elijah and his messianic message are a perfect symbol of our hopes and desires for the world. There is a lovely custom of filling Elijah's cup by having all the participants sitting around the table pour in a little wine from their own glasses, to symbolize that the messianic age of the future will come only if we all contribute our own unique part to making it happen.

### The Values and Ideals We Teach

Passover is a holiday of values and ideals, of hopes for the future and memories of the past. For example, when we retell the story of the ten plagues in Egypt, it is a tradition to remove a drop of wine from our cups at the mention of each plague. This is to remind us that for our ancestors to be free, Egyptians had to suffer as well, and that even the suffering of our enemies, who are also human beings created in the divine image, ought to diminish our own joy as well.

We are also reminded of a well-known midrash (story told by the rabbis to illustrate an ethical or moral point): When the Israelites crossed safely through the Sea of Reeds (some called it the Red Sea) to freedom and their Egyptian pursuers were drowned, they sang a song of thanksgiving to God. According to the midrash, they were joined in their song by the angels in heaven, whereupon God chastised the angels, saying, "How can you sing while my children (the Egyptians) are drowning in the sea?"

This story is yet another reminder of the most important ideals that Passover represents. *We* are not free as long as any man or woman is not free. We can hardly rejoice fully in the defeat of our enemies as long as human beings are made to suffer and remain oppressed.

Passover teaches us that oppression and slavery take many forms in our lives. We are slaves when we feel trapped in jobs that rob us of our sense of self-worth and fill our days with unsatisfying drudgery. We are slaves when we stay in abusive or self-destructive relationships or marriages. We are slaves when we fall prey to addictions of all kinds, whether drugs, alcohol, gambling, or any other self-destructive impulse that we allow to control our lives.

Oppression is found as well in the poverty and hunger that plague the lives of millions throughout the world. As long as people must live each day merely in the pursuit of shelter, food, clothing, the most elemental needs of life, they are slaves. To live in a society in which tens of millions of men, women, and children go to bed each night without adequate health care is to support a system that keeps people from experiencing the fullness of their liberty.

### Personalize Passover

You can personalize Passover in hundreds of ways. The entire family can be involved in creating Passover decorations, Seder plates, cups for wine, or even creative placecards for the table. Family members, no matter how old or young they might be, can help prepare the meal or the special Passover ritual foods.

For example, one of my favorite childhood memories of Passover is helping to grate horseradish for the Seder plate. Yes, it *is* worse than peeling onions, but the tears that came to my eyes were a physical reminder of the tears and suffering of slavery.

Children can help make haroset, by peeling (or eating!) apples, sprinkling in cinnamon, or breaking up walnuts. They can set the table, or help serve the meal itself (one custom is to not serve yourself during Passover, since having another serve you is a sign of freedom).

An excellent way of involving the entire family in discovering the meaning of Passover is to hold up each item on the Seder plate one at a time and ask each member of the family to think of his or her own personal associations or meanings for every symbol. For maror (bitter herbs)—what is bitter in the world today, in your own life or the lives of family or friends? For the shankbone—what are you willing to sacrifice in your life or our world in order to solve some of the world's problems? Also, what is something in your life that is worth sacrificing for?

Hold up the parsley or the egg (both symbols of renewal, spring, and rebirth) and ask, "What has been an experience of renewal or rebirth for you (or us) this year? What areas of our lives are in need of hope and what can we do about them?"

Hold up the haroset (as a symbol of the mortar in the bricks we used as slaves in Egypt) and ask, "What do we use today as our building blocks for the future? What holds our personal relationships or our family together that is important to each of us?"

Point to the salt water and have each person declare anything in his or her life or the world that is worth shedding tears over. How can we make it better, fix the world around us, help to repair torn friendships?

Simple activities such as these, which can be done verbally as you sit at the table, or written down by everyone beforehand and shared as part of the Seder experience, are merely a few examples of the many different ways you can personalize the Passover experience, making it more meaningful and relevant to your own family.

## Shabbat: A Weekly Model of Perfection

When most people think of holidays, they think of a special celebration that comes once a year. Passover and Hanukah are like that, and so are birthdays, anniversaries, and most other festive occasions we cherish. For the Jewish people, however, our most important holiday is one that comes every week of the year. Shabbat, which is the Hebrew word for "Sabbath" (I will use them interchangeably), is the only holiday so important that it is mentioned in the Ten Commandments.

The Jewish Sabbath is traditionally observed on the seventh day of the week, following the biblical commandment "Six days you shall labor and do all your work, but the seventh day is a Sabbath" (Exodus 20:9–10). It lasts from sunset Friday night until sundown on Saturday (or, if you want to get technical, until the appearance of three stars). In fact, all Jewish "days" begin at sunset, based on the fact that the biblical story of creation refers to a "day" using the phrase "And there was evening and there was morning. . . . " Since evening is mentioned first, the ancient rabbis decided that all days should be counted from evening to evening.

Throughout the thousands of years of Jewish civilization, the Sabbath was like a diamond shining in the midst of a field of coal. It was the favorite day of every week, a time when Jews could forget the many difficulties that faced them all week long, put aside their struggles and frustrations, and turn to study and meditation—pursuits that brought them peace of mind, contentment, and joy.

The Sabbath was considered to be such a crucial and sacred time each week that many rabbis taught it was equal in importance to the observance of all the laws of Judaism. It is so central to Jewish life that a great Jewish writer, Ahad Ha-Am, once commented, "More than the Jewish people has kept the Sabbath, the Sabbath has kept the Jewish people."

What is it about Shabbat that has made it unique, sacred, and special for all these thousands of years? The key is found in a famous midrash, in which the rabbis of old invested the Sabbath with the sacred, mystical power to foreshadow the messianic age. The midrash tells the following story:

When God was about to give the Torah to the Jewish people, God summoned the people and said to them: "My children, I have something precious and wonderful that I would like to give you for all time, if you will accept my Torah and observe my commandments."

The people asked, "Ruler of the universe, what is this precious gift that you have for us?"

God then replied, "It is the world-to-come, the messianic age."

The people of Israel answered, "Show us a sample, a model of the world-to-come."

God then declared, "Shabbat is a sample of the world-to-come, for when that world comes, it will be one long Sabbath."

As you can see, the specialness of the Sabbath lay in its role as a symbol of the perfect life, the messianic age when all people will realize their potential, when peace and security, justice and compassion will rule the hearts of all humanity. Shabbat is such a symbol because it provides a weekly reminder that the world *is* perfectible, and that we have the power to create a mini-version of that perfectibility in our own lives today.

The Sabbath has served for thousands of years as a constant reminder that the ideal of a perfect life, a perfect world, is an ideal that *can* be achieved. In Chapter 2 we learned that Judaism has always empowered the individual to believe that his or her own choices make a profound difference in whether the world itself ultimately supports, nourishes, and sustains human life. Shabbat is a weekly model of that empowerment, and a weekly reminder of the importance of the daily choices we make.

It isn't study per se, worship or meditation per se, that matters. It is what they have always represented for the Jewish people that is the key. When a Jewish person spent the Sabbath in study and prayer, it was an experience that reinforced each week the crucial values that underlie all of Jewish civilization. That reinforcement took place simply in the process of participating in a religious service whose prayers spoke about peace, about freeing the captive, healing the sick, clothing the naked, housing the homeless, and bringing justice and compassion into the world.

As the prayers were read or chanted, the lessons and values were reinforced. The same is true when Jews would study the Torah on Shabbat. The lessons they learned had to do with creating the kind of world we all dream of. Thus through worship, meditation, and study, the traditional Jew was able to create a weekly ritual that constantly fortified his or her resolve to help bring about this messianic age which the Sabbath symbolized.

The key for you today lies not necessarily in worship or study themselves (although you might find those ac-

tivities worthwhile as well, provided you seek out a synagogue whose philosophy and approach seem suited to
your needs), but in discovering for yourself and your
family those activities, experiences, projects, and shared
endeavors that will make the Shabbat meaningful and
relevant *to you*. The truth is that Friday night and Saturday will come each week whether you do anything
special about them or not. Making them a *Sabbath* is
totally up to you. If Shabbat is to have any value for
you, it must be found in the opportunity it provides
each week for doing something unique, different, out
of the ordinary that brings an added sense of meaning,
purpose, and ethical values into your life and the life of
your entire family. Each week you get another chance
to create a moment in time that somehow reminds you
that the world *can* be the kind of place we dream of, it
*can* be filled with excitement and creativity, inspiration
and love. What Shabbat teaches us is that in many ways
all of that is up to us. *We* can make a difference in the
quality of life on our little planet, and Shabbat comes
each week to give us another chance to discover how.

To make something "holy" is to set it apart from
other things, to make it special and ultimately important. That is what is meant when the Torah tells us,
"Remember the Sabbath day and keep it holy" (Exodus
20:8). It means that whatever we do to use the Sabbath
as a model of those values and ideals that are of ultimate importance to us *is* what making it "holy" is all
about.

All of us can do that, regardless of religious background, regardless of whether or not we have a Jewish
education, belong to a synagogue, attend religious services, or read the Torah. Each of us has virtually an
unlimited range of possibilities for making the Sabbath

"holy" in his or her own way. And no one can say that one way is better, more acceptable, more "correct," or more appropriate than another. If it accomplishes the goal of serving as a symbol or model of the perfectibility of the world and our power to bring that perfectibility closer to reality, then however we choose to celebrate the Sabbath is the right way.

### The Three Traditional Shabbat Rituals

Naturally, certain rituals for celebrating Shabbat in one's home have become commonly accepted over the course of Jewish history. The three most important take place on Friday night: (1) lighting and reciting a blessing over candles, (2) reciting a blessing over wine, and (3) reciting a blessing over a special Shabbat bread (a twisted egg-bread, called hallah). These three rituals are usually done in the following manner.

#### Lighting Shabbat Candles

It is customary to light at least two candles on Shabbat, although some households light a candle for every member of the family. It is traditional for the woman of the house to light the candles and recite the blessing, although it is perfectly permissible for a man to do it. In many families, one person lights the candles and the entire family joins in the blessing.

When the candles are lit, the following blessing is recited (the Hebrew is found in the glossary at the end of the book):

Blessed are you our God, divine power of the universe, who makes our lives special through commandments, and commands us to kindle the Sabbath lights.

Since lighting the candles marks the "official" beginning of the Sabbath, at the conclusion of the blessing many people wish each other "Shabbat Shalom" (the traditional Sabbath greeting, meaning "Have a Sabbath of peace") or "Good Shabbos" (the Yiddish word for Sabbath).

In many homes, the Sabbath is made more special by setting aside a set of candlesticks that are used only on Friday night. However, you can use any candlesticks, and might even encourage your children to make their own as part of their contribution to making the Sabbath special.

### The Blessing over Wine

The second traditional Friday night ritual involves reciting a blessing over wine (and then drinking it!). Wine is a regular part of every Jewish holiday or special time, because it is a symbol of joy and sweetness. The Sabbath is supposed to be a time of joy, and in fact there is a rabbinic saying, "In the end of time, we will be brought to judgment for all the opportunities for Sabbath joy that we had which we passed up."

Traditionally, sweet red wine is used (for its obvious symbol of sweetness), but since you are drinking it, use whatever wine you like. The special blessing over wine on Shabbat, called the kiddush (which means "sanctification" in Hebrew), is traditionally recited (or chanted) by the man of the house, but can certainly be recited by a woman as well. In many homes, the entire family joins in saying the blessing together. It can be recited in the following manner (the Hebrew is found in the glossary):

Blessed are you our God, divine ruler of the universe, who creates the fruit of the vine.

In some homes, each person has his or her own cup of wine for the blessing, and in others one larger cup is blessed and then passed around for everyone to share. Many families use special kiddush cups made of silver, ceramic, pewter, or glass. Naturally, you can use any cup that is available, since when you use it to bless the wine on Friday night, it automatically *becomes* a kiddush cup for the night. Be creative and flexible. Family members may want to have "their" special cup for the Sabbath, and there are certainly hundreds of ways one might decorate or make a kiddush cup.

One way of personalizing the Sabbath rituals is to have each family member (or friends if they are present) recall one joy from the past week that they are willing to share with everyone. These joys then create an atmosphere of joy and blessings that pervades the entire kiddush experience.

Remember, it is usually best to add one ritual, idea, celebration, or experience at a time to your family's repertoire. In that way no one ritual will seem overwhelming, and you will find it easier to integrate a new ritual into your existing routine.

### The Blessing over Bread

In traditional Jewish practice, every meal begins with a simple blessing over bread. It is this same blessing that is recited on the Sabbath over the hallah (twisted eggbread). Of course, if you don't have hallah, you can recite the blessing over whatever bread you do have. Hallah is available from bakeries and many delicatessens. There is also a delicious frozen hallah dough that you finish baking in your own oven made by a company called Kinneret, which is available in many supermarket frozen food sections.

The blessing over the bread (called in Hebrew the *motzee*, which means "brings forth [bread]") is usually recited by the entire family, or given as an honor to a guest or older relative. The blessing (which is the same one used before any meal, any day of the week) is:

Blessed are you our God, divine power of the universe, who brings forth bread from the earth.

In many families the bread is first passed around and everyone tears off a piece, prior to the reciting of the blessing itself. The custom is to tear the hallah rather than cut it because Shabbat is a time of peace and knives were considered to be instruments of war. Tearing symbolizes our rejection of war and bloodshed, and our desire to create a world free from the need for weapons of destruction.

It is an interesting fact that the Hebrew words for bread (*lehem*) and war (*milhama*) come from the same root. This reminds us that bread—sustenance—has often been the root of war throughout the course of human history. When the day comes that we have created a world providing sustenance for everyone in abundance, perhaps wars will cease as well.

### A Blessing for the Children

Although the three blessings over the candles, wine, and bread form the core of a Friday night Sabbath celebration, *my* favorite ritual involves a blessing over children. A wonderful, loving Jewish custom on Shabbat is that after the other three blessings have been said and before the meal has begun, parents stand over their children (one at a time, if you have several) and give them their own special blessing.

There are traditional words in Hebrew and English that can be recited at this time (found in the glossary), but Didi and I prefer to make up our own blessing for Gable each Friday night that reflects whatever is on our minds that week—just a few words of our own personal dreams, hopes, and desires for our daughter and her life. In that way, each week is unique, and Gable never knows exactly what we are going to say.

This becomes a wonderful opportunity to communicate to your children the values and ideals you think are important. In each week's blessing they hear emphasized over and over again the kind of people you want them to be, the kind of life you want them to lead.

### Do-It-Yourself Shabbat

Shabbat is definitely a do-it-yourself experience. Beyond the traditional blessing opportunities that I have just outlined, the rest is up to you. Your challenge is to find ways of marking the Sabbath that fit your family's lifestyle and needs. No two families are exactly alike, no two have exactly the same background and interests, so it isn't surprising that different families make up their own rules for how Shabbat is going to be celebrated in their home.

My own parents had a rule that all arguments, yelling, and disagreements had to stop when we got to the dinner table on Friday night. In a family with three sisters (two older and one younger), that wasn't always easy!

All of us knew that once we sat down to dinner, we were expected to let go of the rancor we had been carrying around during the preceding week. Shabbat was supposed to be a time of peace in our house (at least for the length of Friday night dinner), and it served as a concrete lesson in how we all *can* control our own emotions enough to live at peace with each other if we so choose.

Having a meal free of discord is one way of creating the Shabbat spirit in your home. After we had all gathered around the Shabbat table on Friday nights, my mother would say a few words about the things she was grateful for that week, her dreams for our family or hopes for the future, as a kind of personal prayer prior to reciting the traditional blessing over the candles. This was just one more simple way of making the Sabbath a special time for all of us, and it took only a few minutes each week to create.

Another custom we have in our own family today is to empty our pockets of change and put it into the family tzedakah box before we light the Sabbath candles. In this way we remember that celebrating Shabbat is a time to rededicate ourselves to sharing our blessings with those less fortunate—only then will the world come closer to its messianic potential.

Be creative and enlist the help of family and friends. Ask the rest of your family to come up with suggestions that you can try for adding something different, special, or unusual to your way of celebrating the Sabbath. You don't have to do the same thing each week; you can try new things or go back to things you used to do that you enjoyed as time goes on.

As always, the most important element is your own involvement and participation in the process of creating the kind of Shabbat experience that you and your family will share. The details of exactly what you do or how you choose to celebrate are far less important than the principle that it is you who are making the decisions.

The Bible tells us, "Rejoice in the Sabbath and call it a delight." The more you make the Sabbath meaningful for you and your family, the more certainly it will become a delight.

## The Ten-Minute Holiday

For many people, the idea of celebrating a holiday that they haven't grown up with is extremely intimidating. They dwell on all the history, rituals, customs, foods, blessings (often in a foreign language), and unfamiliar rites they would have to learn in order to celebrate the holiday the "right way."

Throughout this book, my goal is to make Judaism and the raising of Jewish children as accessible, understandable, and "do-able" as possible, regardless of your background. The most important element is your willingness to try something new, to take it one step at a time, one ritual or activity at a time, according to the pace and level of involvement that fit best into your own life.

Holidays do not have to be elaborate events, filled with religious details and traditional customs. They can be simple, tailor-made activities that you share with your family to mark these special times during the year as significant Jewish moments of celebration.

In fact, every celebration can be a "Ten-Minute Holiday" if you want it to be. Hanukah can be celebrated as simply as lighting the candles in the menorah and reciting together the appropriate two blessings (three on the first night). The blessings can all be written down in advance on individual pieces of paper (or one large sheet that hangs on the wall) so that everyone can easily read them at the appropriate time. This simple ritual takes no more than ten minutes.

If having your own Passover Seder is too intimidating at first, you can simply have a dinner that includes one Seder plate in the middle of the table. If you do nothing more than hold up each item on the plate and repeat what I have written in this chapter about each one, or ask your family to share their own associations with what the items symbolize, you will have acknowledged Passover with another Ten-Minute Holiday.

Every Friday night as you gather at the dinner table, light candles, bless the wine and hallah, and say "Shabbat Shalom," you will have a weekly Ten-Minute Holiday.

Every holiday can be approached initially in exactly the same way. Using the resources in the last chapter of this book, your local synagogue, or a Jewish bookstore, you can find simple children's books on each holiday and create your own Ten-Minute Holiday celebration as you are introduced to the rich and wonderful annual cycle of the Jewish festival year.

Judaism is a civilization that provides you with unlimited opportunities for learning, for celebrating, and for reinforcing in your children the significant values and ideals that guide your life. I hope this book will help you along your own path of Jewish discovery, and will make the celebration of holidays and the Sabbath an exciting and fulfilling experience for your entire family.

# Four

# Mixed Marriage or Mixed Message? Sharing Judaism in an Interfaith Home

*Gandhi said he was Hindu, Christian, Moslem, Jew, Parsi, Buddhist and Confucian. What he was saying was that he recognized truth in all the major religions. While varying in custom, ceremonies, holidays and the vernacular of prayer, all the major faiths agree . . . that the moral law is sacred and should be observed.*

*Rabbi Edgar F. Magnin, at age 94*

Interfaith marriage represents perhaps the biggest challenge today's parents face in successfully raising children with a strong Jewish identity. Every year new studies demonstrate that the rate of interfaith marriage in the Jewish community continues to rise. In fact, in most major centers of Jewish life today, Jews marry non-Jews at a rate of 50 percent or more!

Interfaith parents today are confronted with a whole range of questions and issues that were simply not relevant to most parents in previous generations. Working out differences, respecting the backgrounds and religious choices of both parents and their extended families, creating an atmosphere in your home where such differences are seen as broadening and enhancing the totality of your family's religious experiences are difficult and time-consuming tasks. Yet thousands (if not millions) of interfaith couples are doing just that, every day, with sensitivity, open minds, trust in each other, and a commitment to developing a life partnership that nourishes the emotional, psychological, and spiritual needs of everyone in the family.

If no children were involved, 90 percent of the arguments and disagreements in interfaith relationships would disappear. Usually, adults are able to create relationships based on mutual trust, respect, and tolerance, regardless of their religious backgrounds, by adopting the attitude that they have their beliefs and the person they love has his or hers.

Throw a child into the equation, however, and these same tolerant, flexible, supportive, and understanding adults often turn into hard-core religious/cultural chauvinists, who come roaring out of their respective religious closets as defenders of whichever faith they happen to have been born to. Such parents often surprise even *themselves* with the depth of emotion they feel.

Children bring out the sense of tradition in us all; they stir our ancient longings for immortality and remind us that we are part of a chain of humanity stretching back eons. Our sense of personal history is piqued, and we find ourselves reminiscing about our childhood and planning how to share all the exciting things from our past with our own children.

In the midst of such reveries, however, individuals suddenly realize that their partner may have very different ideas as to the childhood memories he or she wants to share with the same child. That realization begins the process, which for many lasts through the entire childhood of their children, of negotiating the religious lifestyle that will form the center of their children's cultural identity.

Making these child-related decisions is often the single most difficult task that interfaith couples must face. Unfortunately, there are no easy answers, for the world of interfaith marriage is a relatively recent phenomenon, and most couples must struggle to find their way alone. Most couples simply make compromises that will work at the time and hope that things will get smoother as they acquire more experience with the decisions they are forced to make each day, month, and year.

"How do we make child-rearing decisions?" I am often asked. Couples who were raised in different religions often are so timid with each other about the issues of child rearing that, as with so many unexpressed feelings and emotions, they are loath to discuss how they *really* feel for fear of estranging themselves from the person they love. You *must* force yourself to break through this barrier if you find yourself avoiding the conversations that in your heart you *know* are inevitable.

So how do you know whether you are making the right decisions? Most of the time, there is no one "right" decision to be made. There are no magic formulas for raising perfect children, there are only individual human attempts at doing the best you can for their safety, security, health, and emotional well-being.

If parenting courses are available where you live, whether from a college or university extension or a synagogue, I strongly advise you to take them together. Somehow, "Parenting 101" was one of those many crucial courses left out of the standard high school curriculum, so most people have very little real information or helpful knowledge about how to be a good parent. They are simply thrown headfirst into the deep end the minute the child is born, and it's sink or swim for everyone.

## Are Kids Confused by Two Religions?

When it comes to interfaith child-rearing issues, it is often more important *how* discussions take place and decisions are made than the specific content of the decisions themselves. The reality is that such religious issues are decided in different ways by different couples.

Lee and Judy came to a meeting of the minds easily (names are changed throughout this chapter to assure anonymity). "I think it is important for kids to have a basic religious upbringing," Lee told me. "The philosophy of getting along with people and creating the kind of world we want to live in together is something that religion teaches. That, I believe, is the most important thing for kids to learn."

Judy added, "It could be confusing to kids if it's not clear up front. People have said to me, 'You are confusing your kids, having a Jewish mother and a Catholic father, celebrating all those holidays together,' but my children understand our lifestyle and have their heads on straight. I know my kids, and we talk about it often.

"It doesn't confuse them at all. They know who they are, who and what their parents are, what religions we celebrate, and see themselves as the product of parents who are from two different religious traditions. They get to have both of them in their lives if they want, and they see that as an advantage over others.

"When they were younger, they used to say 'I'm half Jewish and half Catholic.' The only decision that we made about religion was to leave it up to them, and make sure they could sample the aspects of our religions that were meaningful to us."

The question persists among interfaith couples as to whether children are confused when growing up in a household that includes more than one religion. In general, it depends on how clearly the religious differences are articulated by the parents, and whether the parents have chosen to give their children a particular identity of their own.

For young children, religious and cultural identities are kind of like name tags—they help give them a sense of belonging to something greater than themselves. It helps them feel connected to a group and literally to feel like they know who they are because they fit in somewhere. Emotionally it matters less which name tag you give them than it does that they have one at all.

I'll never forget the pained look on the face of a young boy when he told me, "I know what my father is and what my mother is, but I don't know what *I* am. It's not good to be nothing, Rabbi."

How poignant, and how true. No one wants to be "nothing," and to the degree that giving your children a religious identity will help them feel they are "something," and a part of a stable, rooted, and secure community, it is an essential component of their positive self-image. My experience counseling hundreds of couples and families has shown me that religious consistency encourages emotional stability in children. It can be Jewish or Christian or whatever, but the key is to give them *some* sense of an identity to hang on to. If you are reading this book, chances are the identity you have decided should be their primary one is Judaism, and this book, I hope, will help you do that successfully.

In many ways, the feelings that children experience about religion, whether Jewish or not, along with their sense of self-identity, are determined primarily by the attitudes and emotional tone conveyed by their parents at home.

Children are confused when parents live lives of denial, confusion, secrecy, and avoidance of religious issues. When parents are open, honest, clear about their own beliefs, values, and patterns of celebration, children grow up with the kind of security and sense of self-worth in the religious realm that is so crucial to the development of their overall self-esteem and knowledge of their place in the world.

I am reminded of Mary, who was the product of a Protestant mother and a Catholic father. The experience of growing up with constant religious tension in her home was so negative for her that when she married a Jewish man as an adult, she was eager to convert to

Judaism to ensure that *her* children would never go through what she had experienced.

"I was really confused as a child," she said. "If I chose to go to Catholic church, my mother would feel hurt, and when I wanted to attend a Protestant church, my father got upset. I was always caught in the middle between them, and as a child wanting to please both parents, it was hell.

"Yes, I was definitely confused by the whole thing, but the confusion wasn't exactly over who I was, it was more a result of the lack of knowing exactly what was expected of me as a child. That was the most difficult part, because I never really knew what I was supposed to believe, think, and do."

Mary's experience is typical of the caught-in-the-middle feeling that plagues many children of interfaith marriages. As a parent, it is your responsibility to give clear direction to your children, to let them know what is and is not expected of them when it comes to belief, religious values, rituals, celebrations, holidays, and the like.

"Leaving it up to them" will work *only* if the environment they are raised in is free of competing religions. It is not always an easy task to give your children the clarity of religious direction that is needed when you yourself are not sure exactly the direction *you* are going.

As Mary told me, "There is a conflict when you see one member of the family always going to church or synagogue and the other never going. It sends you double messages, and as a child you don't know what is supposed to be important and what isn't. Our home was really not a religious home at all. Religion was avoided like the plague, and values were never discussed because they would open up a Pandora's box and lead to a religious discussion that was taboo. Thus I grew up confused over what I was supposed to do about religion, and turned off to it altogether."

Parental expectations obviously play a major role in determining the overall attitudes of interfaith children. Do your children know how you and your spouse/partner feel about their participation in religious rituals, holidays, and celebrations? Do they think that either of you will feel hurt if they express an interest or desire to participate in or learn more about the religion of the other?

Such questions are fundamental to the attitude formation of interfaith children, and you owe it to yourself, your partner, and your children to discuss these issues as fully as possible so as to present a clear and united message to them, one way or the other.

## Should We Let the Children Decide for Themselves?

Conveying a positive attitude about religion and the religion of your partner is one of the most important gifts you can give an interfaith child. It is less important what your respective religious beliefs are than it is to convey to your child respect for each other and each other's beliefs. The most effective parenting occurs when you teach by the example of who you are and how you act, rather than by what you say.

There are many different choices that you could make regarding the religious upbringing of your child. In one sense, inculcating in your child a reverence for life, a sensitivity to the mystery and beauty of the universe around us, and an appreciation for the diversity of religious beliefs that add color and texture to the fabric of modern society *is* instilling a sense of religious values.

Should you let children decide their religious affiliation for themselves? Only if you truly don't care whether or not your children are raised with a sense of religious values and rituals, or whether or not they have a Jewish identity as they grow and mature. I am certain that you wouldn't let them decide for themselves whether or not to learn the alphabet, how to read, or the manners necessary to get along smoothly in society. You recognize that these are important fundamentals of living successfully in the world. If you feel that an appreciation for the miracles of life, the ability to discover godliness in one's daily life, and a recognition that there is a world around us that transcends the ordinary are important attributes for your children to possess, then you will treat the learning of religion with the same respect as for addition, spelling, or writing.

By letting your child decide whether or not to have religion in her life, *you* are deciding "no" for her in advance most of the time. It is the rare child who actually chooses to attend a religious school, chooses to learn about religion and spirituality, or chooses to embrace rituals and religious practices in her life on her own.

I have sometimes seen children choose to attend religious school against the desires of their parents, but it happens only when, through chance, their *peer group* of friends happens to be attending a given synagogue (or church), and they simply want to be with their friends.

Most parents do not really want to leave the decisions regarding the total religious upbringing of their children in the hands of whatever friends the children happen to have at a given moment. In every other area of your children's lives you communicate to them what it is important to know, to learn, and to do. If you let *them* make the choices when it comes to religion, you are telling them that it simply isn't important enough for the adults in their lives to bother with or make decisions about.

## Success Through a Team Marriage

To be successful interfaith parents requires a team marriage, plain and simple. Just as couples are able to work out their differences in other areas of life every day, so too they have successfully negotiated their religious and cultural needs in ways that have created harmony, peace, a sense of mutual respect, and a commitment to the well-being of each partner in the marriage.

In a team marriage, both partners treat each other as an integral and essential aspect of their own life. You know that it is your role to give 100 percent support to the other, because the success of your marriage and your parenting as well demands it. You need each other to provide a safe and secure environment in which to take risks with each other and your child-rearing decisions. In this way you can stretch your horizons to include the experiences and background of the other, and when necessary incorporate them into your life together. Thus the interfaith aspect of your parenting becomes an enriching rather than a divisive element in your marriage.

In the team marriage, you face the world and your children with a partner. You know you are never alone in your decisions because you are committed to meeting each experience, each obstacle, each choice as yet another opportunity to express that partnership. Team marriages grow out of the desire to create a relationship that sets the ideal example for your children of how it is possible for parents, regardless of their individual religious backgrounds, to be mutually supportive and united in their approach to creating the family's cultural/religious lifestyle.

In the best relationships, there is both the recognition that differences in background do exist and the ability to create an atmosphere of mutual respect, tolerance, and cooperation. In such relationships both parties show a willingness to sit down and explore rationally *together* the potential impact these differences might have on their marriage and children.

Such an attitude of mutual respect and support allows the parents to develop clear, simple, workable strategies for helping each other understand and live with these differences in ways that add luster and depth to their lives. Here are a few of the specific strategies I have seen developed by such parents:

- Whenever an argument erupts over a decision based on a difference in background, one party or the other calls "time," and both sit down and write out their feelings and the source of their disagreement as *they* perceive it. They then exchange writings, and by the time they finish reading and commenting on them, they often have cooled down enough to work out a compromise or joint decision that works for both of them.

- At a time when things are going well and there are no outstanding quarrels or disagreements between them, parents may agree on a plan whereby they alternate in decision-making roles regarding religious/cultural differences. "This holiday you get the final decisions, and the next one I get." (Or the children get to vote, or whatever . . . )

- Both partners agree in advance (sometimes in writing) never to allow their own parents (with their different religious backgrounds) to come between them or put them in a position where they feel they have to choose between their spouse and their parents regarding religious/cultural issues as it relates to their own children.

- Both partners may agree to take an Introduction to _____ (Judaism, Catholicism, etc.) class together to learn more about each other's backgrounds. These classes often help clarify which areas of their religion and culture are important to them to pass on in some way to their own children, and which aspects of their "parent" religion they no longer find meaningful.

- Partners may agree in writing prior to the actual marriage itself, or prior to the birth of their children (or *after* the birth of their first child, when these issues suddenly hit them full force), exactly which holidays they will celebrate together as a family. This agreement is often subject to review annually, or at any interval the couple chooses.

- As I have written on many previous occasions, "If at first you don't succeed, talk, talk, talk, talk, talk, talk, talk, talk, talk, talk, talk, talk, talk, talk, until you do."

### Acknowledging Differences

One of the most crucial lessons interfaith couples learn on the road to successful parenting strategies is the importance of acknowledging that differences *do* exist between them. The ability to speak of these differences out loud to each other can be both a liberating *and* a binding experience for both parents, and it is often a necessary prerequisite to developing a successful and supportive team marriage.

So if you have chosen to be part of an interfaith marriage, first admit that the differences are there. Only after you are honest about the differences themselves can you create a way together to transcend them and continue supporting each other in your ongoing quest to build a strong, enduring, loving parenting partnership.

### *Differences as Opportunities*

One thing to keep in mind is that differences are not necessarily barriers to successful parenting. They can be, in fact, *opportunities* for mutual support and decision making. Each parenting issue, whether it is which holiday to celebrate, how to celebrate a holiday, with whom to celebrate, what to tell your children about Jesus, about their own identity, is an opportunity to reinforce the love and caring and essential values that form the foundation of your relationship.

In fact, it is often the way you resolve areas of disagreement and potential conflict in your marriage that serves as the single best indicator of the resiliency and inner strength of the relationship. This once again becomes a model for your own children, and automatically reinforces some of the very values you desire to teach: respect for others and their opinions and backgrounds, history and culture, the importance of caring about the feelings of others, and more.

The challenge of an interfaith marriage is to create harmony out of differences, mutual respect and love in the midst of ambiguity and paradox. It is to see every difference as a window into the unknown world of your partner's past. Each difference you uncover is something you can learn about and from each other as well, adding the unique depth and dimension that only an interfaith relationship contributes to the challenge of parenting.

## Uncovering True Religious Feelings Takes Time

"When we first started dating it was all so exciting and wonderful that it never occurred to me we were different at all," Florence confessed. "I guess I was a bit naive at the time, but I just thought things would continue along in the blissful way that they had started. I thought any differences would melt away like snow in the spring. It's funny how being excited and in love allows you to ignore things that your otherwise rational mind would tell you might just be important some day."

"Yes," Arthur responded, "I felt the same way at first. Like, so what if she's Jewish and I'm Catholic; so what if our parents are different, if we were raised differently. We didn't *seem* very different. You know, there is basically very little difference in the way we live, the values we have, the things that we like to do. The other stuff, like Christmas and Hanukah, Passover and Easter, doesn't seem very important.

"Of course, when we started really getting serious about our relationship, all of a sudden certain things became increasingly important. Like, for example, it never occurred to me that my child wouldn't be baptized. In fact, it seemed so natural and obvious to me that I never even brought it up. Only when Florence's mother men-

tioned something one day about having a baby naming
or a bris with her favorite rabbi when our child was
born did I realize, 'Hey, there just might be a difference
in expectations here that we'd better talk about.' "

"That was really the first major religious argument
we had," Florence said. "I realized that he expected that
*my* child would be baptized, and I said, 'No way that is
happening to any child of mine!' All of a sudden we
began to discover a few hidden, rather strong emotional
attachments that each of us had to our own religious
background without even being aware of it.

"Religion is a funny thing. You don't seem to use it
until you need it. It's something that you take for granted, and most of the time something you rebel against
or argue about with your parents.

"Then out of the blue you get hit with a religion
attack as you are about to get married or you have a
child. Then things that weren't important before all of
a sudden become *very* important to you and sometimes
you don't even know exactly why."

Florence and Arthur are an excellent example of
what I have discovered in many interfaith relationships.
Uncovering one's *true* religious feelings, the differences
that do exist within couples, often takes time to happen.
For many, this realization develops slowly over the years
of their relationship. In fact, I have heard observers of
interfaith marriages comment on the apparent "delayed
reaction" that seemed to take place in an interfaith parent who "suddenly" had a personal religious "revelation" of sorts, and discovered that he really *did* care
about the influence and continuity of his particular religious background after all.

Such revelations are not uncommon and in my experience stem mostly from the confrontation between

an individual and a specific life-cycle event or series of events in which they are or would like to be involved. For example, Florence and Arthur had a perfectly compatible relationship where religious issues were not a problem whatsoever, *until* Arthur was confronted with the normal life event (having a baby) that called forth a perfectly natural religiously/culturally oriented response on his part—namely, "When my child is born I expect that he/she will be baptized."

For some, it takes a series of events over time in their relationship or family life to evoke a strong enough emotional reaction to suddenly plunge the individual and, as a matter of course, the entire family into a kind of religious/cultural crisis. Perhaps it is the participation in a dozen or so Christmas dinners with the in-laws, the tree brightly lit in the background, that finally pushes the Jewish parent's consciousness over the edge of the comfort zone and elicits disturbing feelings of religious betrayal.

Many couples spend a lifetime struggling to understand and integrate the differences between them, searching for the specific magic strategies that will allow them to have their respective religious needs met. It is important for everyone to understand that our "true" feelings *change* over time, along with, it is hoped, the rest of us.

Arthur's true feelings may have been one thing when he and Florence were dating and first married, and legitimately something quite different when their first child was born. That is the way real human beings live in this imperfect world of ours, and it is important to your own peace of mind to accept that reality in yourself and your partner. What is unimportant today may become very important tomorrow, and what is desperately important today becomes something we smile at in disbelief ten years from now.

Discovering your own religious feelings is an ongoing process that involves honesty with yourself and your partner, the willingness to acknowledge that your feelings are legitimate, whatever they may be, and the recognition that yesterday's feelings and needs may not be today's. Only by honestly confronting these feelings and needs can you successfully structure a loving, nurturing interfaith parenting partnership that will allow for your different needs and emotional/spiritual paths to fulfillment and satisfaction.

## The "Hanukah Bush" and the Hanukah/Christmas Dilemma

One of the most sensitive areas of difference in an interfaith marriage reflects the emotional power of religious and cultural symbols. Religion and culture are two prime areas of life that tend to be loaded with emotional buttons just waiting to be pushed, though most of the time we don't even know they are there.

Simply recognizing that these differences exist in our cultural backgrounds is not enough to curb our often irrational and unexpected emotional reactions to religious symbols. Such emotions often lie deeply hidden beneath the years of our life's experiences, which have dulled them and buried them out of sight and sensitivity.

As has been mentioned, it usually takes a specific religious occasion or celebration, life-cycle event, or moment of stress to unearth these deep-seated emotions. Most often they surface at peak holiday times, when emotions tend to run high anyway.

Without a doubt, Christmas and Hanukah represent the most concrete examples of emotional disharmony as a result of differences in religious/cultural upbringing. For many, the issue is whether or not to have a Christmas tree in a home that is predominantly Jewish in tone. This issue often arises with couples who have decided to raise their children with a Jewish identity, but with one parent remaining Christian and feeling a yearning for the holiday symbols of his or her youth.

At times, the discussion may even continue long after someone who was not born Jewish has converted to Judaism. There is just something so powerful about a Christmas tree that it captures the imagination of children for life. Those who have grown up looking forward to decorating it and joyfully opening their presents each year amid its lovely fragrance and beautiful lights often find it extremely painful to eliminate totally from their lives.

It is without question the single most difficult religious/cultural symbol for most who were raised Christian to give up. For many, each December is a time of tension, conflict, guilt, and unhappiness, as they struggle to overcome their feelings of resentment and loss at no longer being able to re-create the most wonderful and positive memory of their entire childhood for *their* children.

What I as a born Jew have found most enlightening about this issue is the discovery that for most of the non-Jews I have counseled over the years, Christmas itself and the Christmas tree weren't primarily *religious* symbols at all. Over and over again I have been told by those born into non-Jewish homes that to them the tree symbolized gifts, giving, warmth, love, family, the joy and excitement of the holiday season, and the expectation of wonderful family dinners filled with laughter and happy, positive memories.

With this as the primary association to the tree, it is little wonder that its absence each year produces such sadness and despondency among so many who are involved in interfaith marriages. Parents want their children to have the same warm and loving experiences that *they* had as children. Many of these parents actually feel they are depriving their children in some profound way of one of the primary joys of childhood.

I have sat with many interfaith couples as they relived the frustrations and arguments they have endured over whether or not to have a Christmas tree in their home. The Jewish partner is usually strongly against it, saying that for him or her it is a clear symbol of Christianity, the birth of Jesus, and a form of emotional betrayal of his or her Jewish roots, even if they were to call it a "Hanukah bush."

The born non-Jew feels mostly a desire to re-create the wonderful memories of childhood, usually with little specific association with Jesus, Christian ideas of messianism, or even Christianity itself. In fact, it is precisely the lack of clear religious associations with the tree for born non-Jews that makes understanding the strong objections of their Jewish partners so difficult.

There is no magical solution to the Christmas tree dilemma. As with other decisions a couple must make in their interfaith lives, deciding whether or not to have a Christmas tree in the home is a matter of expressing true feelings, working together to discover the hidden longings behind those feelings, potential sources of guilt on both sides, and arriving at a decision together that both can live with.

Believe it or not, there have been times when (even though I am a rabbi) I have suggested to a couple that they get a tree and see how they both feel about it.

Usually, the mere realization that it is impossible to re-create your childhood as an adult in such a totally different setting and lifestyle is enough to allow the non-Jewish parent to keep the tree only as a warm memory.

Sometimes, the opposite happens, and both parents find the tree adds a dimension to their holidays that they desire and are comfortable with. Many do make the tree a symbol of the holiday season, and the explanations given to their children range from "It's a part of Mommy/Daddy's childhood that she/he misses and wants to share with you/us," to "We are using the tree as a symbol of the holiday spirit and the holiday season, of light and tolerance and the love of our family," to "The tree is Daddy/Mommy's because he/she is Christian, even though the rest of us are not."

Obviously, if your goal is to strengthen the Jewish aspect of your children's identity, the more you fill their lives with symbols of *Jewish* culture, the easier your job will be. Regardless of how you *individually* or your spouse *individually* explains the presence of a tree in your home during the Christmas season (and you will hear many who totally discount any "religious" connotations to it), to the rest of the world it will remain "a Christmas tree," with all the religious associations that Christmas evokes.

Shakespeare could have been thinking of just this dilemma when he wrote his famous phrase about a rose by any other name smelling just as sweet. Call it a Hanukah bush, a holiday tree, or any of a hundred creative labels, but don't fool yourself into thinking anything other than the truth—that everyone who walks into your home will still go away telling each other, "Did you see the nice Christmas tree they have?"

Here are some examples of how a number of inter-faith couples react to the Christmas season:

"My family always celebrated Christmas, just to give gifts, and Hanukah as well," said Dan, who is Jewish. "We had a tree, too, because it was just a holiday symbol for us."

"The tree isn't really a religious thing anyway," his Catholic wife, Brenda, added. "It's the spirit of the thing that counts. We share both holidays. His mom buys the kids candy and eggs for Easter, too. She just likes any excuse to buy them things. It isn't a religious holiday with my parents, either. I guess it was more so when I was a child, but not anymore."

"We don't celebrate anything in a 'religious' way," said John, who was raised Lutheran. "The holidays are family times, mostly, but we do tell our children about the religious aspects of them, too. Mostly I see them as just our joyous times together."

"The biggest issues with us regarding raising our kids had to do with the celebration of Christmas and whether or not to have a Christmas tree in our house," said Monica, who was raised Catholic. "We decided to have a tree for me. I think it lost its religious meaning a long time ago. For the material aspects of life we celebrate Christmas, and for the religious, Hanukah, and we decorate for both.

"I get angry with people who tell me, 'You shouldn't have a tree in your home.' Even my mother-in-law says something about it each year like, 'I wish you wouldn't put it up.' Before, I tried to discuss it rationally with her, but now I go for the emotional level. I will say to her, 'I enjoy it, it's important to me as a reminder of my own childhood, and that's just the way it is.' It's too bad that religious symbols push buttons so easily for people and they get so agitated about them."

"My brother-in-law doesn't want us to give him a Christmas present and tells us that we shouldn't have a Christmas tree," said Bobby, raised Presbyterian. Added Rita, who was raised Jewish, "We celebrate Jewish holidays religiously, and Christmas as a gift-giving and family time of the year."

"We celebrate Christmas in our home," said Deidre, raised Protestant, "and it seems to offend lots of Jews that we do. I said, 'We had a nice Christmas' to someone in the office who is Jewish, and he got upset because Aron [her husband] is Jewish. Yes, in my religion, it is the birth of Jesus Christ, but it's more so a time of giving, a happy time, and we have a very nice, happy Christmas. My memories as a kid are mostly of filling our house with relatives."

Rick, who is Protestant, told me that the biggest issue in his marriage to Pam, who is Jewish, is whether to have a Christmas tree in their home each year. Even though he doesn't consider himself "religious" as a Christian, he wants to have the tree simply because "it reminds me of kids, family, getting gifts, and all being together. It's not really a religious holiday for me, but I loved having a wonderful dinner together and celebrating peace on earth for everyone."

As you can see, for many interfaith couples Christmas and Easter become times primarily to "have a dinner and celebrate," without any specific religious overtones to the celebrations themselves. What appears to be celebrated is the idea of family, of sharing, of creating a moment in time each year to simply be together in a happy, joyous, festive environment, and perhaps be thankful for all the gifts and blessings we have in our lives.

Carl, raised by a Catholic mother and a Protestant father, and Mindy, raised Jewish, are yet another example of this typical interfaith attitude toward the celebration of holidays. "We don't have any religious symbols in the house, except a mezuzah on the door and a Hanukah menorah," Carl told me. "We celebrate Jewish holidays with her parents, and Christmas at our house, although not religiously. It's really a family and gift-giving time. We try to give our daughter gifts every other night on Hanukah, and then the rest under the Christmas tree."

Although he and Mindy describe their own celebration of Christmas as not "religious," and communicate it that way to their daughter, Carl admitted to me privately that he has a very different perception.

"For me, in my heart, it *is* religious, and so is Easter. They both are in relation to Jesus and his birth, life, death, and resurrection." And yet, as part of the accommodation to the interfaith nature of his marriage, Carl has agreed all along to allow his daughter to "choose" her own religious identity (at age ten she told me that she was Jewish), and consequently kept the "religious" nature of Christmas to himself.

This example may give some clues as to the power and impact of what you teach your children by the religious lifestyle you create in your home, and the way you describe the celebrations and holidays you share. Carl and Mindy clearly taught their daughter that Christmas was *not* a "religious" experience, but rather a kind of general holiday-season celebration. Since she didn't attend a church Sunday school to learn any different, that is exactly how she perceived Christmas in her home, and had no problem at all identifying herself primarily as Jewish.

"I was uncomfortable with the tree, and Christmas made me feel uneasy," said Michael, who is Jewish. "My mother used to say, 'Well, if you start with a tree, then it will be a cross, then pictures in the house of Jesus . . . ', so I think about it each Christmas."

"I wouldn't have a cross in our home either," responded Michael's wife Fran, who was raised Catholic but has since converted to Judaism. "We celebrate all the Jewish holidays and celebrate Hanukah every night. The tree is just part of the fun of the holiday season. The truth is that Michael likes having it, because he never had one as a child in his home and it's fun for him. I can't just drop and forget everything from my past, so we made an agreement. We try to compromise—like I put up blue and white lights on the tree and make Jewish stars to hang on it."

### The "Compromise" of Mixed Religious Symbols

This compromise that takes place in many interfaith homes is an attempt on the part of both partners to be flexible and figure out together how to have a tree for the born Christian while keeping the religious Christological overtones out of it. In fact, the attempt seems to be to create a kind of Jewish version of the Christmas tree that will not offend the born Jew and at the same time allows the born Christian to keep a special holiday symbol from his or her past intact.

Now, I know that many people from both Jewish and Christian backgrounds will read these words and be offended or horrified. They will say, "How can you mix the religious symbols of different traditions together in the same home and not create confusion for everyone

(especially the children) and demean the spiritual content of both?"

From a purely "religious" perspective, there is a
great deal of truth in what they say. I *have* been told by
believing Christians that they take offense at Jews who
feel nothing for the divinity of Jesus "celebrating"
Christmas and putting up Christmas trees in their
homes. They have told me that the evergreen tree is a
symbol of the eternal divinity of Jesus as the savior of
all humanity, and that for Jews to take this deeply religious celebration and turn it into some kind of generic,
plain-wrap holiday is insensitive and offensive.

You may have such people in your own extended
family as well, and it is a good idea to explore with your
spouse exactly what he or she expects the reactions of
the rest of the family to be. That way, you will at least
be prepared for the reactions that your decisions elicit,
and can think through in advance why you are making
these specific choices concerning your religious lifestyle
and be better able to explain them (to yourself, your
spouse, your children, and anyone else) should the occasion present itself.

The tension over Christmas decorations, wreaths,
and especially trees becomes a perennial problem for
many interfaith couples. "The Christmas tree was the
only religious problem we ever had," Adam said. "She
wanted one so badly that finally one year she got one,
but I wouldn't allow a real tree, just a plastic one, and
it didn't make her happy."

"Of course it didn't," Christy interjected. "It didn't
satisfy me at all, and I was really miserable. It just didn't
smell right."

Often couples try to figure out ways to both have a
tree and not have one at the same time. In a sense, that

is what Rick and Pam finally agreed on. "Rick really wants a tree every year," Pam told me. "The kids have received presents for Christmas and for Hanukah anyway, so we decided to have a tree for Rick. Lisa [one of their daughters] feels it would be hypocritical to have a family tree since *we* are Jewish, so we simply say it's Rick's tree.

"The kids are so steeped in their identity that it doesn't really matter or confuse them in any way. Their identity is not dependent upon whether or not we have a tree, since they know it is because Rick has a Christian background and missed it when we didn't have it at the beginning of our marriage."

For some, the issues are easily resolved, and for others the marriage becomes a lifetime of bargaining, negotiating, compromising, giving up, being less than totally happy or satisfied. I believe that in general in relationships, the issue is not compromise or giving up, it is how both parents can have their own needs satisfied and successfully met, while making decisions together as a parenting team regarding how to raise children, what holidays to celebrate with them, and what they will be taught about the holidays they do celebrate.

## Finding Areas to Share

"Holidays seem to be the biggest issue between us," Walter said. "I was born and raised Christian, so all the Jewish holidays are new experiences for me. There is some overlap between them, but sometimes you have to make choices between one and the other.

"As I looked into the historical background of the various holidays, I discovered many of them are connected. That makes it easier for me to accept all the various holidays that we do celebrate."

Walter and Ruth celebrate Passover, for example, with a Seder. They invite all the neighbors to their house and use the Seder experience as an opportunity to discuss the similarities between their Jewish and Christian backgrounds. They have created a celebration of the holiday that serves to bring them closer together each year, rather than pull them apart.

Whether it is Christmas, Hanukah, Easter, Passover, or any other holiday or celebration that you share, the key element is in the *sharing*. The more you know about each other and your respective religious/cultural traditions, the easier it will be to fashion a shared religious lifestyle that you can both pass on to your children. In this way your choices will help bring an added sense of meaning and significance into the lives of everyone in your family, and it will be that much easier to communicate a strong and accessible Jewish identity to your children, even if they have interfaith parents.

As always, the ability to make decisions in a loving, supportive, nurturing, and sensitive environment is often more important than the decisions themselves. Children are not upset by how you choose to celebrate a given holiday, they are upset when the issue of religion, or culture, or celebration itself becomes a source of conflict, tension, anxiety, and aggravation in their household.

Children do not like to see their parents upset or arguing, regardless of the issues at hand. The important thing is not to let your different backgrounds become battlegrounds that force your children to take sides. That is an impossible no-win position in which to place any child, and is one of the cardinal sins of interfaith parenting.

I have counseled interfaith couples, satisfied and happy with their relationship and their parenting decisions, who celebrate all the religious holidays of both; who celebrate primarily the holidays of one or the other; and who pick and choose each year which holidays they will participate in as a family.

Obviously, the specific decisions they make *do* have a significant impact on the health and vitality of their respective religious communities, be they Jewish or Christian. The fundamental composition of the religious communities of America is in the midst of profound change. The breakdown of distinct barriers between communities, which has led to the explosive increase in interfaith marriages in the first place, is also in part responsible for what may emerge as a new religious and cultural reality.

Whether specific traditional religious communities may like it or not, for a significant and growing percentage of both the non-Jewish and Jewish world today, a new confluence of religious and cultural celebration and ritual that incorporates some symbols from both cultures is probably here to stay. For those religious institutions that respond openly and creatively to this new reality, interfaith families may become one of the largest and most interested populations for potential involvement and participation.

Making constructive and positive child-rearing decisions is one of the great challenges of an interfaith marriage. You never have to feel that you are in it alone. Tens of thousands of couples are struggling with exactly the same issues you are facing, and many of them are creating successful, loving, meaningful lives together for themselves and their children.

Keeping your minds and hearts focused on the skills of open communication and the sharing of feelings and needs will help you to be part of the growing legion of successful interfaith parents. Don't be afraid to seek advice and support from outside sources as well, whether it is other interfaith couples, supportive, nonjudgmental clergy, caring friends, local synagogues, or community centers where there may be programs especially designed to meet the needs of interfaith parents.

## When Others Say Your Child Isn't Jewish

The issue exploded forcefully into my life many years ago, with a phone call from an angry and frustrated congregant. "Rabbi," she nearly shouted, "you have to help me. I don't know what to do. Julie's religious school teacher told her in front of the entire class today that since only her father is Jewish and not her mother, *she* isn't really Jewish either. She is hysterical, crying, angry, confused, and I don't know what to tell her. Can I bring her in immediately and have you talk to her?"

Nine-year-old Julie introduced me to the pain and confusion a child of an interfaith marriage can feel at being confronted for the first time with the traditional definition of Jewish identity—namely, a Jew is someone born of a Jewish mother, *period*. Julie is typical of the thousands of young people today whose Jewish fathers and non-Jewish mothers have chosen to raise them with a Jewish identity, send them to Jewish religious schools, belong to synagogues, and celebrate Jewish holidays.

The Jewish world is divided in its approach to interfaith marriages between the more liberal Reconstructionist and Reform movements, on one hand, and the

Conservative and Orthodox movements on the other. Over a decade ago, first the Reconstructionist and then the Reform movement officially adopted a policy known as "patrilineal descent," which simply put identifies children as being Jewish if *either* their father or mother is Jewish and they are raised as Jews.

This was a significant break with the traditional definition that had been passed down for nearly two thousand years without much debate or accommodation to changing realities. With intermarriage between Jews and non-Jews reaching upwards of 50 percent in most metropolitan communities, the more liberal movements within Jewish life felt it was time to responsibly and compassionately reflect the emerging needs of those thousands of Jewish children like Julie whose parents have chosen to make Judaism their primary identity.

Defining Jewish identity solely on the basis of whether one's mother was Jewish may have made sense in an earlier era of great social turmoil and transfer of populations by conquest, when it was perhaps doubtful who the father might be and the only certainty of lineage came from the birthing mother, but such considerations no longer exist in the modern world.

The traditional definition of Jewish identity, however, is still more widely known by Jews of all backgrounds than the more recent acceptance by the liberal Jewish world of patrilineal descent. Many Jews, ignorant of what modern Judaism has declared, will still blindly announce to someone that if her mother isn't Jewish, she can't really be Jewish either unless she formally converts.

It is shocking and confusing to a child like Julie, who has spent her entire life as a Jew, to suddenly be told by someone else (particularly an assumed "authority figure" like a teacher or rabbi), "Sorry, but you're not really Jewish after all." The truth needs to be told simply, directly, and unambiguously: "You are fully and completely Jewish as far as the entire liberal Jewish world is concerned, even though there are some fundamentalist Jews who believe that you can be Jewish only if your mother is Jewish, no matter how you are raised. In fact, those Jews say someone is Jewish if her mother is Jewish, even if she *isn't raised as a Jew*."

In my synagogue (part of the Reconstructionist movement) and in nearly a thousand Reform and Reconstructionist synagogues throughout the world, Julie's full identity as a Jew is without question whatsoever. Yet there will probably be Jews who will continue to view Judaism as somehow a genetic inheritance that only a Jewish mother's genes pass down to her children.

Unfortunately, there are Jews from all backgrounds of life who have their own prejudices about who is and isn't, can and can not be considered Jewish, regardless of birth, regardless of upbringing, and even regardless of a conscious choice to convert as adults.

I recall a disturbing but telling example of this phenomenon from a number of years ago when I was riding in a group taxi to work in New York. Two women (whom I didn't know) were sitting in the car and discussing a particular rabbi and his wife. One said to the other, "Do you know Rabbi So-and-so?" The second replied, "You mean the one who married the shiksa [an uncomplimentary Yiddish term for a non-Jewish woman]?" The first responded, "Yes, but I thought she converted to Judaism even before they met?" To which the second answered, "Oh yes, I heard that too. But you know, once a shiksa, always a shiksa."

To these ladies in the taxi, Judaism was a genetically transferred trait, like brown eyes, blond hair, or straight teeth. No amount of rational discussion, no amount of intellectual explanations to the contrary would make one iota of difference to them or their inbred prejudices.

If you are the child of a non-Jewish mother and a Jewish father, or you have such a child, then you simply have to accept that prejudice, ignorance, and insensitivity come in all shapes, sizes, and religious backgrounds, including Jewish. What is most important is to remember that your identity and the identity of your children do not depend on the acceptance or rejection of the fundamentalist elements of the world Jewish community.

Who you are, who your children are, is a result of how you live your lives, how you define *yourselves*, whether or not you feel connected to and a part of the greater Jewish world. That is why I always identify three categories of Jews: Jews by chance (born Jewish), Jews by choice (converts to Judaism), and Jews by association (born non-Jews who are living with, related to, and feel a part of the extended Jewish community).

I do believe that it is a good idea to discuss these differences in perception within the Jewish world with your children so they will know what to expect and not be devastated by a casual remark from a thoughtless person. The Jewish world is complex, with even the most Orthodox, fundamentalist Jews arguing among themselves over fine-line distinctions and definitions of what is kosher, proper, correct, and acceptable within Judaism. For many such fundamentalist Jews, even I and the thousands of rabbis like me who have been ordained by the Reform, Reconstructionist, and Conservative movements are not rabbis at all. So you can see how important it is not to let other people's narrow-mindedness determine your own sense of Jewish identity or self-worth.

Because Judaism is the total evolving religious civilization of the Jewish people, no one group, movement, or community has any more "official" status or standing than any other. Certainly there is no single authoritative voice in the Jewish world (as the pope might be in the Catholic world) who is empowered to make official pronouncements concerning proper Jewish observance, dress, ritual practice, or identity.

Part of the greatness of Judaism lies in its flexibility and openness. You and your family *are* a part of the ongoing evolution of the Jewish civilization each time you celebrate a holiday in your own way or add your own unique nuances to Jewish rituals and customs. Your Judaism must be meaningful and valuable to you and your life on your own terms. Of course, the more you learn about Jewish tradition, history, and customs, the more fully you will be able to participate in Jewish life, and the more meaningful your participation will probably feel to you.

Regardless of your background, the ideal in Judaism is a commitment to lifelong learning. Whether you were born Jewish, are a Jew by choice, or are a Jew by association, I believe the richness and grandeur of Jewish traditions can add something powerful, spiritual, valuable, and, yes, sacred to your everyday life. I encourage you to continue taking each step along that path to enhanced purpose, meaning, and fulfillment within Jewish life for you and your family.

# Five

# The Synagogue Dilemma: When, How, and Whether to Make Organized Religion a Part of Your Child's Life

*Deep in the heart of both critical Christian and alienated Jew, there is something that says there is more to Jews than meets the eye. There is a mystery about the Jews ... and within this mystery lies the reason for the folk pride of the house of Abraham.*

*Herman Wouk*

One of the most striking distinctions between Judaism and other religious groups is that what binds Jews together in their identity is not primarily *belief* but *belonging*. It is the sense of belonging to a community, a people, a culture, a common history, and an ancient civilization that provides the primary focus and strength of Jewish identification, no matter where in the world Jews are found.

This strong sense of identification with the *community* of the Jewish people has been the one constant emotional and sociological anchor throughout Jewish history. Religious "beliefs" have varied, theological concepts have undergone transformations and evolution, but the commitment to peoplehood and community has continued as the common thread that binds all Jews into a single cloth.

In many ways, *community* is the essence of Judaism. That Jews experience themselves not only as the descendants of the biblical Abraham and Sarah, Moses, Miriam, and King Solomon, but as literally part of an enormous extended family that today stretches to every continent of the globe is central to any understanding of Judaism and Jewish life.

Two thousand years ago, the great sage Hillel said: "Don't separate yourself from the community," and his words have been taken to heart by Jews throughout the world ever since. That is undoubtedly why Jews have been so successful at creating a wide variety of institutions to meet the needs of such a diverse Jewish population.

The Jewish community has created and supported everything from philanthropic organizations, museums, hospitals, and institutions of higher learning to social service agencies, communal defense agencies (to battle

145

against prejudice and bigotry), and synagogues. All of these and more are involved with strengthening the daily life of Jews of all ages emotionally, socially, ethically, and spiritually.

In this chapter I will provide you with a brief overview of the role of the synagogue in the life of the Jewish community, discuss some of the factors that might go into making a decision about affiliating with a local synagogue, and give a thumbnail sketch of the various synagogue movements and what distinguishes one from another.

## Where Did Synagogues Come From?

The word *synagogue* is derived from the Greek *synagoge*, which means "assembly" or "congregation." It was without question a revolutionary institution in the history of religion. Synagogues probably first appeared as the result of the Jewish exile from Israel to Babylonia around 586 B.C.E., when Jews were taken far away from the religious center of their civilization in Jerusalem.

The practical reality of living in exile and desperately wanting to maintain the continuity of their religious connection to life "back home" forced the Jews of Babylonia to search for spiritual substitutes for the physical offerings and sacrifices they were unable to make. Out of this adversity came the revolutionary notion that "offerings of the heart" could take the place of the lambs and bullocks of the traditional sacrificial system. In this way, the institution of personal and communal prayer was first established, and the synagogue as a separate institution was born.

When Jews were once again allowed to return to Israel after this first exile, they had developed an attachment to the idea of communal worship, and brought it back with them. Thus by the time the Romans destroyed the temple in Jerusalem in the year 70 C.E. and drove the majority of Israel's Jews into an exile that would last some two thousand years, the synagogue as an institution was already waiting in the wings to take its place of prominence.

Today synagogues are created by their own members as independent institutions to serve the needs the members define. No hierarchy that dictates policy from on high, or forces individual synagogues to accept the decisions of others as binding. Each synagogue is empowered to adopt the prayerbook of its choice, to establish its own bylaws, rules, standards, and curriculum of religious instruction, and to hire its own professionals (like the rabbi and cantor) at its discretion.

Naturally, national organizations of like-minded synagogues have emerged over the years and formed "movements" that reflect particular Jewish ideologies, philosophies, theologies, and practices. Even so, these movements are voluntary associations whose members primarily adopt "guidelines" as suggestions of standards that ultimately are up to individual synagogues to follow or not as they choose.

As we shall see, the synagogue is a multifaceted institution. Whether it's a small, intimate group of families who meet to worship, study, and pass on their heritage and culture to their children, or a formal institution with thousands of families and a large professional educational, administrative, and spiritual staff, it remains a voluntary association of families who have joined together to express their identity and help each other find greater purpose and meaning in life.

## The Synagogue Is More
## Than a Place to Pray

When most people think of a synagogue, they think of people going to religious services to pray. That is perfectly logical for two very good reasons: First, as you just learned, the synagogue's original purpose was to substitute for the previous system of worship that centered around animal sacrifices; and second, in the modern world, prayer, worship, and the celebration of holidays with religious services *are* among the most important of the various functions synagogues continue to serve in the life of the Jewish community. In reality, however, a synagogue is much more than simply a place to pray.

If the truth about Jewish life were told, almost anyone who has ever been a member of a synagogue (with perhaps the exception of Orthodox synagogues) would acknowledge that praying is *not* why most people join in the first place. In fact, as a rabbi who has spent nearly twenty years serving in various synagogues, it is my studied opinion that attending services and praying per se is one of the *least* important motivations for most members' synagogue involvement.

If you were raised in a Christian home, you may find this puzzling. When teaching about Judaism to people with non-Jewish backgrounds, I've discovered that they inevitably have a difficult time understanding why more Jews don't attend services, how it is that so many Jews who belong to synagogues are hardly ever there, and why such a large percentage of Jews don't belong to any synagogue at all.

The reasons, as we have discussed earlier, have their origins in the fact that Judaism is an evolving religious civilization, *not* a narrowly defined system of religious beliefs. Since Jewish identity does not depend on the acceptance of a specific predetermined creed, many Jews feel no particular compulsion to demonstrate their Jewishness on a regular basis by echoing that creed in the context of religious services.

People belong to a synagogue today because over the centuries of Jewish life it has developed into an institution that satisfies a wide variety of cultural, spiritual, educational, and social needs. Throughout the Jewish world and across the entire spectrum of Jewish observance and affiliation, the synagogue has grown to represent three primary functions, each represented by one of the three Hebrew names by which a synagogue is known: *bait tefilah*—a house of worship; *bait knesset*—a house of assembly; and *bait midrash*—a house of study.

### The Synagogue as a House of Prayer

As I have already mentioned, the synagogue is primarily known to most in its function as a house of prayer. Depending on the synagogue itself and its specific community of members, worship services will be conducted on Shabbat every Friday night and Saturday morning, and in many synagogues every weekday morning as well.

Most non-Orthodox synagogues hold services in both English and Hebrew, with the mix depending on the customs of the individual synagogue, who is leading the services, the specific prayerbook being used, and the movement the synagogue belongs to.

When deciding whether to join a particular local synagogue, it is a good idea to attend several different services so you can see what they are like, whether all are the same, whether they vary from week to week, the general tone, and how comfortable you and your family will be in that particular setting. It is also very helpful to introduce your-self to whoever is leading the services and find out what style of worship is typical of that synagogue. For example, some are more formal, others informal; some use choirs and organs, others use guitars and folk instruments; some use only professional rabbis and cantors, others use lay members of the congregation and community as well.

Prayer in Judaism is both an intensely personal and communal activity. Most prayers in the Jewish liturgy speak in the first person plural: "we." Given the tremendous importance Judaism places on community, it is little wonder that Jewish liturgy has developed as a way not only of linking the individual with the divine, but of linking the community together as well.

Jewish prayer is generally for the good and welfare of the community as a whole, for society as a whole, and for the world and all humanity as well. We pray in the hope that the power which animates life and continues to daily renew the act of creation will inspire all human civilization to recognize the godliness within us all so that we might create a world that supports, sustains, nourishes, and empowers everyone.

To discover this source of inspiration is one of the reasons Jews come together to create synagogues. Whether at a weekly service on Shabbat or as part of a celebration of a significant holiday during the year, religious services serve both to strengthen individual spirituality and commitment to the ideals of godliness and to reinforce our connection to other members of the greater Jewish community.

### The Synagogue as a House of Assembly

The second major role of the synagogue is as a focal point for Jewish social interaction. The synagogue traditionally has functioned as a kind of community center, where Jews gather to socialize, discuss significant issues affecting their lives, ensure that those in need are taken care of, and experience a sense of commonality and connection to each other.

One of the reasons people join synagogues is for a feeling of belonging to something greater than their individual family. They are motivated by the need for connection to others, the need to feel that their lives are not circumscribed merely by the tiny confines of their own homes, but that there is a place where they fit within the larger community.

This "community center" function has always been one of the most important services synagogues provide. In the past, when Jewish lives were threatened, when Israel was under attack, when the world was at war with itself, when traumas of one kind or another struck the community, it was to the synagogue as a center of Jewish communal life that people turned. There they gathered, there they sought solace, comfort, and connection with others.

So, too, on an individual level. One example is how many members of my congregation have commented that they never realized how important the synagogue was to them until someone in their family died. In most synagogues, as in my own, people respond with love, support, food for the mourners and their families, help with whatever chores might need to be taken care of, and, when necessary, financial assistance to ensure both the dignity of a proper burial and the survival of those left behind.

This realization that others are there for you, care what happens to you and your family, and will provide a support system to respond in times of crisis is a prime benefit of synagogue membership.

### The Synagogue as a House of Study

The third major function of the synagogue is as a house of study. Jews have been known as "the people of the book," in part because learning, study, and education have always been such fundamental values in Jewish life.

Most people know that the primary transitional puberty rite for a young boy or girl in Jewish culture is the bar or bat mitzvah ("bar" for boy, "bat" for girl). The essence of this ceremony, which takes place at about age thirteen, is that the young man or woman leads the congregation in prayer, then reads or chants from a section of the Torah scroll in Hebrew.

Think for a moment of what this teaches about the values of Judaism and the Jewish community. When a man or woman comes of age in America, the three primary symbols of that change of status are (1) he or she can now legally drink alcohol, (2) he or she can now vote, and (3) he or she can now legally gamble.

In Jewish culture, the symbols of transition from childhood to maturity are (1) the young person can assume the responsibility for leading the congregational prayers, (2) he or she is expected to fulfill the ethical and ritual responsibilities of Jewish adults, and (3) he or she has *studied* sufficiently to be able to read and teach from the most sacred texts of the Jewish people, the Torah scroll.

It is study, learning, teaching, and transmitting ethics, values, and tradition from one generation to the next that have been most revered in Jewish life. That is why to be a scholar, to be a professional, to be educated has long been prized in Jewish society. It is no coincidence that some 90 percent of all Jewish college-age children go to college. Study, not only for its role in preparing one for the challenges and responsibilities of life but also for its own sake, is one of our most important and cherished values.

The synagogue has always been the center of Jewish study; learning, both for children and adults, is an integral part of every synagogue program. In fact, Judaism has not put its educational emphasis merely on the teaching of children, but regards the concept of lifelong learning as the ideal. That is why every synagogue has a program of adult or continuing education, along with a curriculum of religious and cultural instruction for children.

In deciding which synagogue your family might join, you should find out about the range of educational opportunities offered, what the tone and educational goals of the religious school are, the kinds of texts and materials that are used, the backgrounds of the teachers and their particular religious orientation (how traditional they are, what they teach about God, about interfaith marriage, about relations between Jews and the non-Jewish world), and the philosophy of the educational director and rabbi.

## Why People Join Synagogues

It should be obvious by now that there are many reasons people might join a synagogue. Some join because they are searching for a place to discover God and spirituality. They seek a common community of faith where Jewish worship and prayer throughout the year can give them a sense of spiritual rootedness, inspiration, and peace.

Some join synagogues because they are seeking connection to a greater Jewish community. They want to feel that they belong, to develop and nurture friendships and relationships with others, and to have a base from which to get involved in broader community issues such as housing the homeless, feeding the hungry, seeking peace and justice in the Middle East, improving the quality of life in their own community, state, and country.

Others join synagogues in order to learn more about what it means to be a Jew, and to have a place that will assist them in passing down the important values of Jewish life to their children. They want their children to have a strong sense of who they are, a good Jewish self-image, and the opportunity to develop the basic Jewish life skills that will allow them to feel at home in any Jewish community where they might find themselves in the future.

Many parents join synagogues initially to take advantage of the religious education that the synagogue provides for their children, only to find that by the time their children are through with *their* Jewish education, the parents have become interested *themselves* in Jewish learning and study. Such people often continue their synagogue affiliation primarily to take advantage of the adult educational opportunities (often including bar or bat mitzvahs for adults who never had one as a child), and for furthering their own Jewish identity and education through study and discussions.

You must investigate the synagogues in your own area, speak to the professionals who work there, get to understand their philosophy and theology, their approach to Jewish life and learning, and, perhaps most important of all, get to know the people who make up the synagogue community.

No matter how inspirationally the rabbi might speak or how beautifully the cantor might sing, they are not the synagogue. It is the people who make up the community, the members themselves, who, just like you, have sought out and joined a synagogue for their own reasons who are most important. They are the ones with whom you and your children will interact socially, educationally, and spiritually. It is essential, therefore, to feel comfortable with the members of the synagogue, to feel that they are the kind of people you would like to spend some time with, and whose children you would like to be friends with your own.

Each individual synagogue has its own ambiance, its own emotional tone, its own style and feeling. It isn't enough to paint each institution with the broad strokes of the specific movement it belongs to, either, since the autonomy of synagogue life encourages every one to have its own unique identity.

Even so, there are distinctions between the movements that are important. Not only do their theologies differ (and as a result, each uses its own unique prayerbook), there are significant philosophical differences as well that set one apart from the next. To help with your decision making regarding synagogue affiliation, I offer the following thumbnail sketches of the four major movements in contemporary North American Jewish life, in chronological order of their appearance on the world scene. These same movements are present in countries outside North America, but may be referred to by other names.

## Orthodox Judaism

In one sense, there are only two kinds of Jews: Orthodox and everybody else. Orthodox Jews are generally the most traditional in practice, although what sets them apart fundamentally from everyone else is that they are the only "Torah from Sinai" Jews. According to Orthodox Judaism, a divine being (called Adonai in Hebrew, or God in English) literally dictated the entire Torah to Moses on Mount Sinai, along with all its commentaries and future interpretations. Because the Torah was divinely revealed by God, Jews are obligated to follow every word and to understand them literally as if God were speaking them to us today.

For Orthodox Jews, life centers around the performance of 613 mitzvot, or commandments, which God has given us to follow. By performing the mitzvot faithfully, we are fulfilling God's plan for the universe and keeping our part of the divine covenant first made between God and Abraham, our original ancestor.

Both ethical laws and rituals laws are equally binding within Orthodoxy, and only the most learned and respected of rabbis can offer new interpretations or understandings of how one is to follow Jewish laws and fulfill the commandments. It is often called "Torah True Judaism" by its adherents, as Torah is the ultimate arbiter of what is right and wrong as well as of all personal actions.

Orthodox Judaism expects strict adherence to all the Jewish laws that govern daily life, obviously including such things as dietary laws as well. Strict observance of the Sabbath is expected, which precludes riding, working, lighting of fires, cooking, carrying, and a host of other activities. The day is spent in rest, study, worship, and visiting family and friends (within walking distance).

Orthodox religious services are conducted entirely in Hebrew, no musical instruments are allowed, and men and women sit separately. Women are not permitted to read from the Torah scroll, nor are they counted as equal to men in matters of ritual or as witnesses to Jewish legal proceedings.

Although there are a few ultra-Orthodox groups who have opposed the establishment of the state of Israel on the grounds that only God can reestablish a Jewish state and not human beings, the vast majority of Orthodox Jews are strong supporters of Israel. In fact, in recent years, the largest numbers of North American Jews to immigrate to Israel have been Orthodox Jews who consider all of Israel to be given to the Jews by God (as written in the book of Genesis in the Torah).

Within Orthodoxy itself there are differences and gradations of observance and philosophy. Some of the ultra-Orthodox still maintain the unusual dress of their European past: black coats, hats, and pants, white shirts, uncut beards and sidecurls. Women dress very modestly and when married keep their heads covered.

Orthodox Jews believe that their form of Judaism is the only true, authentic Judaism and that all others are illegitimate. Other movements are not recognized as valid expressions of Judaism, and their rabbis and cantors are often held as illegitimate as well. Orthodox Jews consider the conversions of other movements to be invalid, and would require a second conversion under Orthodox auspices before agreeing to accept a convert as Jewish.

## Reform Judaism

Reform Judaism began in Germany at the beginning of the nineteenth century as a reaction to the traditional Orthodoxy of its time and as an expression of some Jews' desire to bring their Judaism more forcefully into the modern world.

As Jews were struggling to be accepted into contemporary nineteenth-century society, they wanted an enlightened form of Judaism that would be able to adapt to the changing world. They demanded that worship services be conducted primarily in the language they spoke and understood, introduced the use of musical instruments, shortened the service, and included weekly sermons (instead of the traditional twice a year on the Shabbat before Passover and Yom Kippur).

Reform Judaism declared the equality of men and women in Jewish ritual matters, encouraged both boys and girls to have a religious education, and instituted the group ceremony of confirmation to serve as a form of spiritual graduation for both (originally to replace the male-only bar mitzvah). In addition, the Reform movement was the first to ordain women as rabbis and invest them as cantors.

Reform Judaism also introduced the late Friday evening service (instead of the traditional brief service at sundown), and seated men and women together (instead of separately as in Orthodoxy).

A fundamental principle of Reform Judaism is the notion of individual autonomy—that every Jew is entitled to decide for himself or herself which rituals, customs, and Jewish laws he or she will follow. Contrary to the "Torah from Sinai" approach of Orthodoxy, Reform Judaism (as with Reconstructionist and Conservative Judaism) believes that the Torah was created over time by individual human beings who passed it down first orally, and eventually in written form, until it came to be accepted as "sacred."

Because Reform Judaism rejects the divine authorship of the Torah, it relegates all ritual laws of Judaism to a matter of personal choice by individual Jews. Some traditional Jewish practices (such as dietary laws and rit-ual purity and cleanliness) were declared out of date and obsolete and are generally no longer observed by Reform Jews.

Reform Judaism places its primary emphasis on eth-ics rather than ritual. It revived the notion of "prophetic Judaism" and focuses on the great ethical ideals found in the writings of the biblical prophets. Much of the energy of the Reform movement as expressed through its national organizations (see Chapter 7) has been di-rected toward social action, community involvement, and general human rights issues and matters of con-science.

Within the Reform movement, too, there is diversi-ty and disagreement. On such issues as officiating at interfaith marriages or the degree to which Hebrew, *kipot* (head coverings), and traditional rituals ought to be reintroduced into Reform Jewish practice, there is often heated debate. Even so, the Reform movement champions the freedom to make changes according to the individual dictates of conscience and sees the reli-gion of Judaism as constantly open to change and adaptation.

## Conservative Judaism

Conservative Judaism began as a reaction to what were perceived as the excesses of Reform Judaism. The foun-ders of the Conservative movement believed that Re-form Judaism had tossed out too much of Jewish tradition and law and wanted to find a middle path be-tween the old world and the new. They called their movement "positive historical Judaism," and saw it as "reform tempered by conservatism."

Conservative Jews hold that Jewish law is binding, even though they do not believe it was set for all time at Mount Sinai. They invest the authority for making decisions regarding proper Jewish behavior with a committee of rabbis, who deliberate on questions of Jewish practice and then set policy for the movement.

Much more traditional in its approach to Jewish custom, ritual, law, and practice than Reform Judaism, Conservative Judaism uses much more Hebrew in the service, expects observance of the laws of Shabbat and Jewish dietary laws, and purposely makes changes slowly and with great deliberation.

As a result of the influence of Rabbi Mordecai Kaplan (see Reconstructionist Judaism), who taught for fifty years at the Rabbinic Seminary of the Conservative movement, Conservative Judaism has adopted an approach that emphasizes the idea of peoplehood and the importance of the world Jewish community. Unlike the Reform movement, Conservative Judaism has always stressed the cultural and national aspects of Judaism as well as the religious in its definition of Judaism and Jewish life.

Within the Conservative movement are many who are much closer to Orthodoxy than they are to Reform. For example, the questions of whether to ordain women as rabbis (which they now do, over the objections of these more traditional voices) and to allow women cantors into the Conservative cantors' association became bitterly fought ideological battles within the movement. Conservative Judaism shares with Reform and Reconstructionism the idea that its purpose is to harmonize traditional Jewish religion and culture with the demands of modern science and the scientific realities of contemporary society.

## Reconstructionist Judaism

Reconstructionism, the newest of the four major branches of modern Jewish life, is the only movement that began in the United States (the others all started in Europe). Its philosophical basis is found in the writings of Mordecai Kaplan, who defined Judaism as the evolving religious civilization of the Jewish people (an approach you will find familiar from reading this book). He taught that Judaism encompasses art, history, culture, literature, music, language, homeland, customs, laws, and community—in short, all the elements we normally associate with any civilization.

Reconstructionism emphasizes community and peoplehood, and vests authority in the decisions of the individual community as it struggles to set standards and guidelines for its members.

Several issues clearly set Reconstructionism apart from the other movements in Jewish life. First is the rejection of the traditional idea that Jews are a "chosen people." Reconstructionism believes that such an idea is not only arrogant and promotes anti-Semitism and intergroup disharmony, it simply isn't rational or logical.

Reconstructionism believes that every people, every culture, every religious group chooses its own unique path to answering the same ultimate questions of life: How do we discover meaning and purpose in the world? What is the meaning of creation? Where did we come from, and where are we going? How can we create a world of peace where individuals and nations can sit down together in harmony and goodwill?

Furthermore, to believe in the idea of a "chosen people" implies that God is a supernatural being who can "choose." Reconstructionism totally rejects this notion;

it is in its understanding of theology where Reconstructionism clearly stands apart from other movements.

Reconstructionists believe that God is simply the term that we use to refer to the highest ideals and values to which we devote our lives. God is not an external "being" that acts upon us, but rather a power that works through us. God is the power or process through which we achieve individual fulfillment, and is discovered in the everyday miracles of life.

Since God is a power or process and not a being, it is impossible to be "chosen," or to see the Torah as divinely dictated to Moses on Mount Sinai. For Reconstructionists (as for Reform and Conservative Jews), the Torah is the record of the Jewish people's spiritual history and search for meaning in life. We read it like spiritual poetry, and see it as a reflection of our ancestors' search for God in their own way and on their own terms.

Reconstructionism is perhaps the most aggressive champion of the equality of men and women within Judaism (and the only movement whose rabbinic association has had several women rabbis as president), and it pays conscious attention to the development of Jewish rituals and ceremonies for various nontraditional family settings.

Reconstructionists introduced the ceremony of bat mitzvah, the idea of Jewish community centers, Havurot (small Jewish fellowships), and a new prayerbook, which is the first in Jewish history to be created by a commission composed equally of men and women, rabbis and nonrabbis. Most Reconstructionist services have more Hebrew than is typical in Reform services, and less than Conservative services.

Reconstructionism believes that one of the primary functions of Jewish ritual is to join Jews together in a strong sense of community. Therefore, there is a commitment to retain as much of Jewish ritual as can be made relevant to the lives of modern Jews, in order to strengthen the bonds of peoplehood and our connection to the world Jewish civilization.

Israel has always been a central element in Reconstructionism: it is seen as the spiritual and historical homeland of the Jewish civilization. In fact, the first symbol of the Reconstructionist movement was a wheel with Zionism as the hub, religion, culture, and ethics as the spokes, and the communities of the Diaspora as the rim.

Reconstructionism believes that Judaism must constantly be evolving to meet the needs and demands of every age, and that it is the responsibility of individual Jews to be full participants in this process. Its ideal is a pluralistic democratic model, whereby all Jews would join together in each community to provide for their common spiritual, emotional, physical, and educational needs.

Regardless of the label an individual synagogue might have, or the specific movement to which it might belong, each community is unique, with its own special tone and flavor, and each reflects the personalities that make it up. That is why as you search for the answers to whether or not to join a synagogue and which synagogue to join, you must allow yourself and your family to try them on for size. Visit different synagogues and speak to people who attend them. Ask questions of the professionals, the active members, and the not so active as well.

As with Judaism itself, synagogues are there for you and not the other way around. The fundamental building block of the Jewish community, they have been responsible for maintaining Jewish life and culture for thousands of years across the globe.

The synagogue of your choice ought to be a place where every interaction encourages you to return for more. Each time you participate in a service, a celebration, a class, a program, a concert, or a lecture, you ought to feel that something has been added to the richness of your life and the life of your family that you simply cannot get in any other setting. I know that it can be so, particularly if you are willing to participate yourself in making it happen.

# Six

# Building Your Child's Jewish Self-Esteem

*In Israel, in order to be a realist you must believe in miracles.*

*David Ben-Gurion*

*The treatment of the Jews in every country is the thermometer of that country's civilization.*

*Napoleon Bonaparte*

When all is said and done, perhaps the single most important challenge of raising Jewish children in our contemporary world is to successfully build their Jewish self-esteem. How can you reinforce the positive nature of their Jewish identity? What can you do to counteract the anti-Semitism and negative stereotypes of Israel, Jews, and Judaism that are still so prevalent in this primarily Christian world? How can you nurture within your children a feeling of pride in being part of a unique civilization that has contributed to the world far beyond what its meager numbers would suggest is possible?

One of the things I remember clearly from my childhood is the constant reference Jewish adults were always making to whether or not a famous, scientist, doctor, inventor, or entertainer was Jewish. "You know he/she is Jewish" was like a badge of honor that made the famous even *more* famous, and any celebrated personality even more valuable in my eyes.

Everyone likes to be part of a winning team. "Pride of association" is a well-documented motivational technique, and I believe that Jews have unconsciously recognized and successfully used this basic psychological reality for decades (if not centuries) to help instill in our children a strong sense of pride in membership in the Jewish people.

"You mean *they* were Jewish too?" is a comment that can't help making your children feel good about themselves as they link their own identity and understanding of their place in society with that of a noted inventor, actor, humanitarian, or musician. During my childhood years, being aware of who was Jewish and who wasn't *did* make me feel proud to be a part of a people who have contributed so much to the progress of Western civilization.

This isn't to say that in order to feel good about the successes and contributions of your own culture or civilization, you must harbor any negative feelings or derision toward the culture or civilization of anyone else. It simply provides you with an opportunity to reinforce the positive self-image of your children *as Jews*, in a world that is sometimes hostile to Jews.

When your children begin reading biographies, make sure they read about famous Jews in history as well. Point out to your children that the three most influential thinkers of the twentieth century have been Jews: Albert Einstein, Sigmund Freud, and Karl Marx. This is something they can feel a justified sense of pride about.

When, as a child interested in baseball I heard that Sandy Koufax had refused to pitch in a World Series game because it fell on Yom Kippur, the holiest day of the Jewish year, I felt a sense of pride that he was one of us, and willing to stand up for what he believed in.

When I learned that Jonas Salk, who invented the polio vaccine that saved tens of thousands of lives, was Jewish, I was even happier to pop that little sugar cube into my mouth, and feel good that a Jewish person like me had made such a major positive contribution to the world.

When I laughed at the Marx Brothers, heard the incredible voice of Barbra Streisand, or watched Leonard Bernstein conduct the New York Philharmonic with his unmistakable flair, I was proud that I, too, was a Jew like them.

Pride in the accomplishments of Jews, as individuals and as a people, can help reinforce in your own children the importance of the unique heritage in which they are being raised.

Not everyone will agree that pointing out positive Jewish role models to your children is a good way to reinforce their Jewish self-esteem. Some might feel that such pride is really a form of cultural arrogance and affected superiority over others. I suppose it's like the age-old Jewish joke in which the rabbi, after listening to the complaint of one neighbor against another, says, "You are right." The second neighbor then explains his position, and the rabbi also says, "You are right." At this point his wife, who has been listening from the next room, comes in and says, "But they can't *both* be right." The rabbi thinks for a moment about his wife's words and replies, "You know, you're right too!"

I believe it is something to be proud of that, as I noted previously, 27 percent of the Nobel prizes awarded to American scientists have been won by Jews, even though we are less than 3 percent of the population. I believe it is something to be proud of that nearly everyone in the world today is affected in one way or another by the revolutionary changes in how we perceive the human mind that was Freud's gift and in how we understand the very nature of energy and matter that was Einstein's.

The fact that so few in number have had such a giant impact on the world has intrigued and puzzled commentators of all religions and nationalities ever since the Jews gave the Bible and the inspirational ethics of its Ten Commandments to the world.

Of course, there have been Jewish gangsters, murderers, racists, and scoundrels, as well. There are people we can be ashamed of; certainly no country, people, or civilization is without blemish or above reproach. But I see nothing wrong with focusing on the outstanding individuals Jewish civilization has produced, and using these individuals to serve as inspirations and sources of self-esteem for your children.

When Elie Wiesel wins the Nobel Peace Prize, or Isaac Bashevis Singer receives the Nobel for literature, or Betty Friedan is honored as the "founding mother" of modern feminism, or Natan (Anatoly) Shcharansky becomes the international symbol of the struggle for human rights and resistance to the oppression of totalitarian regimes, or Paul Simon brings 750,000 ecstatic fans to their feet singing with one voice "Bridge Over Troubled Water," I am proud to be a Jew like them.

Building your own child's Jewish self-esteem is a process of positive Jewish association. For some families it becomes a kind of "Jewish identity game," in which the challenge is to be the first to announce that a famous individual in any field is Jewish too. It is a simple yet powerful way of encouraging a feeling of connection between your child and talented people who are Jewish (how about Billy Crystal or Whoopi Goldberg, Barbara Walters or Dr. Ruth Westheimer, Woody Allen or Ted Koppel . . . ), and is another way of communicating that to be a Jew is to be part of an illustrious extended family. Just as you would feel proud of any family member who becomes famous or has a significant impact on society, so too all Jews become by extension part of your family as well.

## Anti-Semitism and Jewish Survival

"It is for his virtues, not his vices that the Jew is hated," wrote Theodor Herzl, the founder of modern Zionism. Although the premise of this claim might be argued back and forth, no one doubts the fact that prejudice, bigotry, and discrimination have been part and parcel of the Jewish experience ever since we first were dragged into exile over two thousand years ago.

Anti-Semitism, an irrational antipathy to Jews and Judaism, is still part of the reality of Jewish life today, as it has been for centuries. Raising Jewish children in our contemporary world requires that they understand the broader implications of their Jewish identity and recognize that there may always be people in the world who would hurt them, defame them, insult them, or attack them for no reason other than that they are Jews. Since anti-Semitism is in many ways a nonrational response of the often ill-educated and uninformed masses, it can be frustrating to try and explain to your children *why* it exists in the first place.

Whether you live in North America, Europe, or the Far East, South America, the Middle East, or the Soviet Union, what your children need to learn about anti-Semitism can unfortunately be summed up in two words: It exists.

Having grown up in the United States in the fifties and sixties, I have undoubtedly lived in one of the least discriminatory, least anti-Semitic societies in the history of the world. Yet I can remember the emotional stress I experienced in elementary school, when all the other children (except two Asian kids and me) left class to go to "release time" for Bible study in a trailer parked in front of the school.

I remember dropping out of my Boy Scout troop because there were too many anti-Semitic remarks made by a number of the more popular boys in the troop. I recall being beaten up on my paper route one day by a couple of kids who "didn't like Jews." An incident here, an incident there, and I got the message that there are always a few around, even in America, who won't like you because you are a Jew.

The term *anti-Semitism* was apparently coined by Wilhelm Marr, a German racist who established the "Anti-Semitism League" in 1879. This was a shift from the past, when anti-Jewish sentiments were directed at Jews primarily for *religious* reasons. The official Christian church, relying on the Gospels of Matthew and Mark in the New Testament, denounced the Jews for "killing" Jesus, and declared that, having rejected the true religion, the Jews were now abandoned by God, thereby deserving punishment and castigation.

With the coming of Christianity to the Roman Empire, Jews were stripped of political, economic, social, and religious rights, and it became accepted among the nations to stigmatize and denounce Jews at every turn. Jews were segregated in ghettos (the word *ghetto* itself comes from the Italian word for "foundry," which was the primary landmark in the section of Venice where in 1516 the Jews were first forced to live apart from the rest of society), severely restricted from participating in "Christian" occupations, forbidden to own land, and obliged to engage in trades (like moneylending) that others saw as noxious and offensive.

Over the centuries, Jews have been tortured, forced to convert, massacred by crusaders, raped, and exploited. They were expelled from England in 1290, France in 1306, Austria in 1421, Spain in 1492, and Portugal in 1497. In the past, this treatment was simply accepted as part of the natural order by societies whose Christian doctrines demanded that the Jews be perceived as having fallen from God's grace. In that context, whatever pain and suffering were visited upon them were a kind of divine retribution for refusing to accept Jesus as God's anointed savior.

This "religious" anti-Jewishness gave way to a more ethnic, social, and cultural anti-Jewishness in the seventeenth and eighteenth centuries. By the time Wilhelm Marr came along with his Anti-Semitism League in 1879, anti-Jewish political parties had proliferated throughout Europe as well. This phenomenon led directly to the establishment of Hitler's Nazi party in Germany, and glorified the notion that anti-Jewishness was based on racial and biological inferiority. The "racial" basis for hating Jews was particularly pernicious, since it necessitated the actual destruction of the Jews, given that mere conversion or assimilation would only disguise their inherent biological inferiority.

This litany of anti-Jewishness is not designed to depress you or imply that the world is hopelessly hostile to Jews. In fact, the world we live in today is blossoming with freedoms never before imagined on earth. In country after country across the globe, where there was once repression and fear, there is hope and liberation. This is clearly the most exciting time imaginable to be alive, and the most dynamic and opportunity-filled moment in the history of the world in which to raise your children as well.

Yet manifestations of anti-Semitism can still be found in America today. The Anti-Defamation League (ADL), a Jewish watchdog agency that documents overt acts of anti-Semitism such as vandalism, graffiti, swastika scrawling, attacks on Jews, and the comings and goings of anti-Jewish hate groups in America, reminds us each year of the thousands of complaints it receives of such hostile acts in communities both large and small. In his recent book *Chutzpah*, celebrity lawyer Alan Dershowitz writes of receiving "almost daily anti-Semitic missives" in the mail, and reminds us how often anti-Semitism masquerades today as "anti-Zionism."

Martin Luther King, Jr., hit the nail on the head years ago when he said, "When people criticize Zionism, they mean Jews; you're talking anti-Semitism." Such an equation is most obvious in the Soviet Union, where blatantly anti-Semitic books, magazine articles, and political tracts have simply been replaced in the language of today by substituting "Zionism" every time it used to say "Jew."

It is ironic that one of the first public demonstrations to take place as a result of the newfound freedoms of expression in the Soviet Union was an anti-Semitic rally by the ultranationalistic group called Pamyat.

In their published literature, Pamyat called upon the Soviet people, " . . . for a fight against the threat of Zionism. . . . The Zionists are plotting a takeover of Russia . . . Nazism was born out of Judaism!!! [emphasis theirs] . . . Nazism has jumped out of the Talmud . . . How long can we put up with dirty Jews, who have brazenly infiltrated our society . . . " And this in the late 1980s, when "new" anti-Semites were now claiming it was the "Zionists" who brought Communism to Russia, ruined the economy, and even caused the disaster at Chernobyl.

And what about living in America? In the land of equality, the closest we have ever come to a Jew running for president was Kitty Dukakis; nor has there ever been a Jewish vice president or chief justice of the Supreme Court (in fact, despite all the Jewish lawyers in America, we don't even have a Jew *on* the Supreme Court), and every year there is an attempt by the Christian right to establish Christianity as the "official" religion of America.

So what do you tell your children about anti-Semitism? You tell them that, unfortunately, the world still has people in it who are ignorant, prejudiced, bigoted, stupid, mean-spirited, emotionally insecure, and foolish. Many such people hate others as a way of feeling better about themselves.

Whether bigotry is aimed at people of color, people who speak a different language, people with disabilities, short people, fat people, young people, old people, or Jews, it inevitably reflects the bigot's lack of feelings of self-worth. Hatred and prejudice need no reason other than they somehow make the one who hates feel superior. They follow no logic, require no facts, and don't even need the object of the bigotry and hatred to be present.

For example, in the midst of the reawakening freedoms and national fervor of Eastern Europe, Jews have somehow once again become the targets of attacks, accusations, and slander, in spite of the fact that hardly any Jews remain in any of the countries involved. In Romania, where the number of Jews is minuscule, a political candidate can still be defeated by his opponents claiming a hidden "Jewish" ancestry. In Poland and Hungary, Czechoslovakia and Romania, half a century after the genocidal policies of Hitler and Nazism have all but eliminated every trace of Judaism and Jews, it is once again popular to speculate that "Jews create an anti-Semitic atmosphere in order to get into the limelight."

Your children need to be aware of the reality of bigotry and anti-Semitism, as they ought to learn (at an appropriate age) of the horrors of the Holocaust. Part of the process of developing Jewish self-esteem is the ability to stand tall in the face of persecution. The Haggadah on Passover says, "In every generation tyrants have risen up to destroy us," and yet we are still here. Mighty nations have come and gone, empires have risen and crumbled, but the Jewish civilization lives on.

At the same time, it is important to keep anti-Semitism in America in perspective. Without question, Jews in the United States today live in the most free, most tolerant, most accepting, least prejudiced, and least anti-Semitic country in the world. It is a country with no official anti-Semitism, a small (even when vocal) minority of hatemongers, and a vast number of non-Jewish politicians, religious leaders, writers, and journalists willing to speak out forcefully for justice, morality, and decency whenever necessary.

A wonderful example of such support came in the form of an editorial in the Colorado Springs *Gazette-Telegraph* by the non-Jewish journalist William Aiken, following a flurry of Nazi scrawlings on synagogues and other public buildings:

> JEWS GO HOME . . . Well, this is nothing new. Never in the past have you ever taken this gentle suggestion to move on. But heaven forbid, suppose just this once, you thought that expression of a few sick people actually expressed the conviction of all the people in this wonderful land of ours, and all of you started to pack your bags and leave for parts unknown.
>
> Just before you leave, would you do me a favor? Would you leave your formula for the Salk vaccine with me? You wouldn't be so heartless as to let my children contract polio? . . . And please have pity on us, show us the secret of how to develop such geniuses as Einstein and Steinmetz and oh, so

many others who have helped us all. After all, we owe you most of the A-bomb, most of our rocket research and perhaps the fact that we are alive today, instead of looking up from our chains and our graves to see an aging, happy Hitler drive slowly by in one of our Cadillacs.

On your way out, Jews, do me just one more favor. Will you please drive by my house and pick me up too? I'm just not sure I could live too well in a land where you weren't around to give us as much as you have given us. If you ever have to leave, *Love* goes with you, *Democracy* goes with you, everything I and my buddies fought for in World War II goes with you. God goes with you. Just pull up in front of my house, slow down, and honk, because, so help me, I'm going with you, too.

There is a great sense of pride in knowing that we live in a country that produces testamonials like this. Obviously, no type of persecution is ever good. But the Holocaust visited upon the Jews by Hitler and the Nazis of Germany was unique in the annals of history. Though others were killed while fighting and in concentration camps, only the Jews were systematically singled out for *total* destruction. It was a war against every Jewish man, every Jewish woman, and every Jewish child, with the aim of eliminating all Jews from the face of the earth, simply because they were Jews. No other people has had to endure such a fate, and with pride you can teach your child that no other people has *survived* as we have either.

Indeed, being proud to be a Jew includes pride in our survival and rebirth. Jewish folk wisdom has always claimed it was better to be the victim than the victimizer. Perhaps that is true, since the victimizers may keep their lives but lose their souls. For Jewish kids growing up today, the most important aspect of understanding anti-Semitism, anti-Zionism, or anti-Jewishness is that we are *not* powerless anymore. In America we have *equal* rights with every other American, and have the responsibility to defend and protect those rights.

On the world scene, we have earned our rights through the amazing story of Israel and her heroic struggle to survive against overwhelming odds. Israelis are like modern-day Maccabees: Though surrounded and greatly outnumbered by the enemy, they have continued not only to survive, but to thrive and to prosper.

## Israel: Rebirth of a Miracle

The great medieval Jewish philosopher Moses Maimonides once said, "Miracles do not come to show us what is impossible, they come to demonstrate what *is* possible." That is why I began this chapter with the quote from Israel's first prime minister, David Ben-Gurion: "In Israel, in order to be a realist you must believe in miracles."

Who could turn on their television set in the spring of 1991 and watch Israel rescue the *entire Jewish population of Ethiopia*, flying 15,000 black Jews who trace their ancestry to King Solomon and the Queen of Sheba to safety in a span of twenty-four hours, and not be moved to tears? One witness commented that it was probably the first time in history that blacks were taken out of Africa to freedom and not to slavery. And it was Israel that did it. Who could see Soviet Jewish families reunited after years of separation and oppression, hundreds of thousands who discovered the quiet flame

of Jewish identity still burning in their hearts after nearly seventy-five years of Communist rule, and not be
moved to tears? And it was Israel that did it.

All these people found a new home; all these people
were reunited with family; all these people were saved
from oppression and welcomed with jubilation and
open arms, because Israel exists. Only since the establishment of the State of Israel in May 1948 has there
been one little place on this entire earth where any Jew
could go, regardless of age, regardless of profession,
regardless of skin color, whether rich or poor, in sick-
ness or health, and *know* that he or she would be truly
welcomed, cherished, considered part of the family.
That is why Israel is the rebirth of a miracle.

The State of Israel was the Jewish phoenix, rising
out of the ashes of the Holocaust. It was the safe haven
for the downtrodden, the oppressed, the tortured, the
weary, and it has always been a beacon of light and hope
in an often dark and troubled Jewish world. For many
Jews, Israel represents our ultimate triumph over the
attempted genocide by all the Hitlers of history. For
others, it represents an opportunity for Jews to normal-
ize, to be a nation like others within the world community, to shed centuries of powerlessness and rootlessness
and feel self-sufficient, self-assured, and able to defend
ourselves.

It is impossible to understand Judaism today, or to
raise children with a strong Jewish identity, without ap-
preciating the unique role that Israel plays in the hearts
of Jews throughout the world. When Scud missiles fall
in Tel Aviv, Jews in Los Angeles, Toronto, and Buenos
Aires tremble, hold their breath, and pray that no
one will be hurt. When images of Israeli soldiers striking Palestinian demonstrators flash on our television

screens, Jews in Houston, London, and Mexico City worry about how Jews and Arabs can ever live together in peace, and the impact that prolonged war, occupation, and the battle against terrorism has on the emotional well-being and soul of Israelis.

Israel is the only nation on earth whose very existence is constantly called into question, whose enemies for nearly half a century have been clamoring for its total destruction, and whose people must live each day under threat to their very survival. For Jews throughout the world, Israel's struggle for existence and survival is their struggle as well.

Israel holds a unique place in the international community. Although it is one of the tiniest countries in the world (about the size of New Jersey), hardly a day goes by without a story concerning Israel making its way onto the front pages of the world's newspapers. It is as if a kind of mass obsession with every detail of Israeli life has taken over the world, as it puts the Jewish state under the magnifying glass of public scrutiny and debate like no other nation on earth.

When the United Nations passed its infamous "Zionism is a form of racism" resolution in 1973, Jews throughout the world were outraged. Here was anti-Semitism written on a global scale, with our most prestigious international body succumbing to the moral debasement of Arab propaganda and hatred. It was an example of how the best way to legitimize anti-Jewishness today is to cloak it in anti-Israel verbiage.

In spite of the passions and support among Jews that Israel's founding engendered, there are still many raised in unaffiliated Jewish families who know very little about Israel, and have only the vaguest notion of what Zionism is all about.

Quite simply, Zionism is the national liberation movement of the Jewish people. It grew out of the Jewish longings of two thousand years of statelessness, of wandering from country to country across the globe without a home. Like other liberation movements, it began formally in the latter part of the nineteenth century, when the idea of self-determination for all peoples grew to become an accepted idea among the nations of the world. So, too, the Jews sought, fought for, and won the right to a homeland of their own on the very soil where Abraham had once walked and David and Solomon had reigned.

The remarkable ability of Jews in Israel to transform the desert into a blooming, thriving country is legendary. Draining swamps and turning them into farms, building world-class hospitals, research institutes, and schools, making orchards blossom where once only sand blew—all have been part of the miracle of the rebirth of Israel in our time.

Despite all its political problems, Israel remains one of the greatest sources of pride for Jews in every country of the world. In fact, for many Jews in America, Israel has become their surrogate source of ethnic identity and the primary cultural focus of their Jewishness. They send their kids to Israel for the summer as to a Jewish summer camp, to experience their roots, connect with their heritage and history, and strengthen their Jewish identity and commitment. While often not supportive of their local synagogue, such Jews instead contribute to the United Jewish Fund, which raises money for Israel to help with immigration, absorption, and social services.

According to the United Nations decision in 1947 to end the British mandate, Palestine was to be partitioned into two states, with Israel to be established as a Jewish state alongside a second Arab (Palestinian) state. The 1948 war between Israel and her Arab neighbors (Israel's "War of Independence") was totally the result of the Arab nations' refusal to accept Jewish sovereignty over *any* part of Palestine, and refusing to establish an Arab Palestinian state as well. They attacked the newborn state with the public intention to "Murder the Jews." Fortunately, when the dust settled, Israel had survived the combined forces of all the surrounding Arab armies, but the Arabs (who had control of the West Bank and Gaza until 1967) refused to allow the establishment of a Palestinian state alongside any Jewish state—it was all or nothing.

This refusal to accept the existence of the Jewish state of Israel by every country in the Middle East (except Egypt, with the courageous decision of Anwar Sadat, who was subsequently assassinated) has been at the root of the Arab-Israeli conflict ever since. The Arab countries refused to allow displaced Palestinians to be absorbed or assimilated into their countries, keeping them in degrading camps, refusing citizenship and equal rights, and using them as pawns to manipulate world public opinion against Israel.

After forty-three years of Israel's existence, the Arab states that surround her have *still* not reconciled themselves to having a Jewish neighbor, forcing Israel to spend a vastly disproportionate percentage of its national budget on defense, creating a constant atmosphere of tension, readiness for war, and fear of terrorism on a daily basis.

When Scud missiles fell on Israel in 1991, Palestinians cheered. The anger, frustration, and lack of realistic expectations for national self-determination on the part of Palestinians on the West Bank and Gaza today after twenty-four years of Israeli occupation is completely understandable. Regardless of where your sentiments lie on the political spectrum, the strength and well-being of Israel in the future clearly lie in a satisfactory resolution, first, to the lack of official recognition and normal relations with neighboring Arab states and, second, to resolving the Palestinian problem in a mutually satisfying manner.

What is important as a parent is to do what you can to see that as your children grow they feel an attachment to Israel as part of their Jewish family. Israel is one of the primary sources for creative Jewish culture in the world today. Your children can read about it, see films about it, hear its music, learn its dances, and participate in the celebration of Jewish life and creativity that Israel represents, totally apart from any particular political issues of the moment.

Visit Israel and learn about its people and culture. Go to see the magic and wonder of Jews of every color, size, and country of origin speaking a hundred different languages (yet all speaking Hebrew), the thousands of Ethiopian Jews mingling with the thousands of Soviet Jews as they adapt to their new Jewish home, and you and your children will experience an unbelievable thrill and sense of belonging to a people that transcends space as well as time.

I want to end this chapter with a wonderful story that captures for me the hope for Israel's future. It is a true story of two human beings from opposite sides of the struggle, and can serve as a symbol of what could be, if only . . .

When the old and new cities of Jerusalem were reunited in 1967, a recently widowed Arab woman, who had been living in Old Jerusalem since 1948, wanted to see once more the house in which she formerly lived. Now that the city was one, she searched for and found her old home. She knocked on the door of the apartment, and a Jewish widow came to the door and greeted her. The Arab woman explained that she had lived there until 1948 and wanted to look around. She was invited in and offered coffee. The Arab woman said, "When I lived here, I hid some valuables. If they are still here, I will share them with you half and half."

The Jewish woman refused. "If they belong to you and are still here, they are yours." After much discussion back and forth, they entered the bathroom, loosened the floor planks, and found a hoard of gold coins. The Jewish woman asked the government to let the Arab woman keep her gold, and permission was granted.

The two widows visited each other often, and one day the Arab woman told her, "You know, in the 1948 fighting here, my husband and I were so frightened that we ran away to escape. We grabbed our belongings, took the children, and each fled separately. We had a three-month-old son. Unfortunately, I thought my husband had taken him, and he thought I had. Imagine our grief when we were reunited in Old Jerusalem to find that neither of us had taken the child."

The Jewish woman turned pale, and asked the exact date. The Arab woman named the date and the hour, and the Jewish woman told her, "My husband was one of the Israeli troops that entered Jerusalem. He came into this house and found a baby on the floor. He asked if he could keep the house and the baby, and permission was granted."

At that moment, a twenty-year-old Israeli soldier in uniform walked into the room, and the Jewish woman broke down in tears. "This is your son," she cried.

And the aftermath? The two women liked each other so much that the Jewish woman said to the Arab mother, "Look, we are both widows living alone. Our children have grown up. This house has brought you luck, and you have found your son, or our son. Why don't we live together?" And they do.

Yes, there is always hope for the future. By teaching our children such stories as this, we remind them that Judaism celebrates the dignity and humanity of everyone, regardless of race, regardless of religion, and regardless of whether or not they are our friend or our enemy.

Building your child's Jewish self-esteem is a challenge no less than any other aspect of child rearing. It requires a clear communication of the reality of Jewish life in the world today, with its frustrations and its successes, its tragedies and its triumphs. There is so much to be proud of in being part of the Jewish civilization of the end of the twentieth century. Share with them the stories of Jews who have made significant, wonderful contributions to the quality of life on our planet, and they will feel proud to be Jews.

Stay engaged and involved with the Jewish community, whether through centers, synagogues, Havurot, federations, social service agencies, or educational institutions. All of Jewish life is yours for the asking, and all is part of your children's inheritance. Give them the blessings of community, allow them to feel the security and rootedness of being connected to a spiritual and cultural civilization that throughout its long history has strived to be a light unto the nations. If you accomplish that, you will then be able to pass on to others the joy and satisfaction of raising Jewish children in our contemporary world.

# Seven

# Where Do You Go from Here?

*The Hebrews have done more to civilize men than any other nation. If I were an atheist, and believed in blind eternal fate, I should still believe that fate had ordained the Jews to be the most essential instrument for civilizing the nations.*

*John Adams*
*Second President of the United States*

This book has been written to make Judaism, Jewish civilization, and the passing down of Jewish culture and heritage to your children as accessible and "user friendly" as possible. In this chapter I will mention a number of resources, both to help you on your path to personal connection with the Jewish community and to help you in the challenging task of raising Jewish children in a contemporary world.

The following is a selected bibliography of books that relate to the ideas presented in the previous chapters. This is by no means an exhaustive list. It barely scratches the surface of the vast amount of information written about the various aspects of Jewish civilization and is to be taken merely as suggestions for the interested reader.

## Bibliography

### Chapter 1   Judaism as an Evolving Religious Civilization

Bamberger, Bernard J. *The Story of Judaism.* New York: Schocken, 1964.

Borowitz, Eugene B. *Choices in Modern Jewish Thought: A Partisan Guide.* New York: Behrman House, 1983.

Dimont, Max I. *Jews, God, and History.* New York: Signet, 1962.

_____. *The Jews in America.* New York: Simon & Schuster, 1978.

Kaplan, Mordecai M. *Judaism as a Civilization.* Philadelphia: Jewish Publication Society of America and Reconstructionist Press, 1981.

Kertzer, Morris. *What Is a Jew?* New York: Collier, 1973.

Kushner, Harold. *Who Needs God?* New York: Summit Books, 1989.

Soncino, Rifat, and Daniel B. Syme. *Finding God.* New York: Union of American Hebrew Congregations, 1986.

Steinberg, Milton. *Basic Judaism.* New York: Harcourt, Brace and World, 1947.

Wouk, Herman. *This Is My God.* New York: Simon & Schuster, 1959.

### Chapter 2    How to Raise Ethical Jewish Children

Adar, Zvi. *Humanistic Values in the Bible.* New York: Reconstructionist Press, 1967.

Cone, Molly. *Who Knows Ten?* New York: Union of American Hebrew Congregations, 1965.

Diamant, Anita, and Howard Cooper. *Living a Jewish Life.* New York: HarperCollins, 1991.

Jacobs, Louis. *The Book of Jewish Belief.* New York: Behrman House, 1984.

Karp, Abraham J. *The Jewish Way of Life.* Englewood Cliffs, N.J.: Prentice-Hall, 1962.

Kurshan, Neil. *Raising Your Child to Be a Mensch.* New York: Atheneum, 1987.

Siegel, Danny. *Munbaz II and Other Mitzvah Heroes.* Spring Valley, N.Y.: Town House Press, 1988.

_____. *Gym Shoes and Irises.* Spring Valley, N.Y.: Town House Press, 1982.

### Chapter 3    Celebrating Holidays and the Values They Teach

Cashman, Greer Fay. *Jewish Days and Holidays.* New York: SBS International, 1979.

Goodman, Philip. *The Hanukkah Anthology*. New York: Jewish Publication Society of America, 1976.

—————. *The Passover Anthology*. New York: Jewish Publication Society of America, 1961.

Heschel, Abraham J. *The Sabbath*. New York: Farrar, Straus and Giroux, 1975.

Knobel, Peter S. *Gates of the Seasons: A Guide to the Jewish Year*. New York: Central Conference of American Rabbis, 1983.

Marcus, Audrey F., and Raymond A. Zwerin. *But This Night Is Different*. New York: Union of American Hebrew Congregations, 1981.

—————. *Shabbat Can Be*. New York: Union of American Hebrew Congregations, 1979.

Millgram, Abraham. *Sabbath: The Day of Delight*. New York: Jewish Publication Society of America, 1944.

Schauss, Hayyim. *The Jewish Festivals: History and Observance*. New York: Schocken, 1973.

Strassfeld, Michael. *The Jewish Holidays: A Guide and Commentary*. New York: Harper & Row, 1985.

Syme, Daniel. *The Jewish Home*. New York: Union of American Hebrew Congregations, 1988.

## Chapter 4 Mixed Marriage or Mixed Message? Sharing Judaism in an Interfaith Home

Cowan, Paul, and Rachel Cowan. *Mixed Blessings*. New York: Doubleday, 1987.

Gruzen, Lee F. *Raising Your Jewish Christian Child*. New York: Dodd, Mead, 1987.

Kukoff, Lydia. *Choosing Judaism*. New York: Union of American Hebrew Congregations, 1981.

Reuben, Steven Carr. *But How Will You Raise the Children?* New York: Pocket Books, 1987.

Sandmel, Samuel. *When a Jew and Christian Marry*. New York: Simon & Schuster, 1978.

Weiss-Rosmarin, Trude. *Judaism and Christianity: The Differences*. New York: Jonathan David, 1965.

## Chapter 5   The Synagogue Dilemma: When, How, and Whether to Make Organized Religion a Part of Your Child's Life

Alpert, Rebecca, and Jacob Staub. *Exploring Judaism: A Reconstructionist Approach*. New York: Reconstructionist Press, 1985.

Borowitz, Eugene. *Reform Judaism Today*. New York: Behrman House, 1983.

Gordis, Robert. *Understanding Conservative Judaism*. New York: KTAV, 1978.

Grunfeld, Isadore. *Judaism Eternal*. London: Soncino Press, 1956.

Kaplan, Mordecai M. *Judaism as a Civilization*. New York: Jewish Publication Society, 1932, and Reconstructionist Press, 1981.

Philipson, David. *The Reform Movement in Judaism*. New York: KTAV, 1967.

Sklare, Marshall. *Conservative Judaism: An American Religious Movement*. New York: Schocken, 1972.

## Chapter 6    Building Your Child's Jewish Self-Esteem

Boxer, Tim. *The Jewish Celebrity Hall of Fame*. New York: Shapolsky, 1987.

Bush, Lawrence. *Rooftop Secrets and Other Stories of Anti-Semitism*. New York: Union of American Hebrew Congregations, 1989.

Chafets, Ze'ev. *Heroes and Hustlers, Hard Hats and Holy Men*. New York: William Morrow, 1986.

Cone, Molly. *The Mystery of Being Jewish*. New York: Union of American Hebrew Congregations, 1989.

Frank, Anne. *Anne Frank: The Diary of a Young Girl*. New York: Doubleday, 1967.

Goldberg, M. Hirsh. *The Jewish Connection*. New York: Stein & Day, 1976.

Greenberg, Martin H. *The Jewish Lists*. New York: Schocken, 1979.

Gross, David C. *Pride of Our People: The Stories of One Hundred Outstanding Jewish Men and Women*. New York: Doubleday, 1979.

Hertzberg, Arthur. *The Zionist Idea*. New York: Atheneum, 1959.

Oz, Amos. *In the Land of Israel*. Philadelphia: Jewish Publication Society, 1987.

Prager, Dennis, and Joseph Telushkin. *Why the Jews? The Reason for Anti-Semitism*. New York: Simon & Schuster, 1983.

Wiesel, Elie. *Night*. New York: Avon, 1972.

## General Interest

Bial, Morrison. *Liberal Judaism at Home.* New York: Union of American Hebrew Congregations, 1971.

_____. *Your Jewish Child.* New York: Union of American Hebrew Congregations, 1978.

Borowitz, Eugene. *Liberal Judaism.* New York: Union of American Hebrew Congregations, 1984.

Dershowitz, Alan M. *Chutzpah.* Boston: Little, Brown, 1991.

Einstein, Stephen J., and Lydia Kukoff. *Every Person's Guide to Judaism.* New York: Union of American Hebrew Congregations, 1989.

*Encyclopaedia Judaica.* Jerusalem: Keter. 1971/72.

Johnson, Paul. *A History of the Jews.* New York: Harper & Row, 1987.

Kushner, Harold. *When Children Ask About God.* New York: Reconstructionist Press, 1971.

Polish, Daniel; Daniel Syme; and Bernard Zlotowitz. *Drugs, Sex, and Integrity, What Does Judaism Say?* New York: Union of American Hebrew Congregations, 1991.

Strassfeld, Sharon; Michael Strassfeld; and Richard Siegel. *The Jewish Catalog.* Philadelphia: Jewish Publication Society, 1973.

Telushkin, Joseph. *Jewish Literacy: The Most Important Things to Know About the Jewish Religion, Its People, and Its History.* New York: William Morrow, 1991.

*The Torah: A Modern Commentary* (commentaries by W. Gunther Plaut and Bernard J. Bamberger). New York: Union of American Hebrew Congregations, 1981.

The more informed you are about the nature of the Jewish community, and the issues that are important to it, the easier it will be for you to communicate to your children where they fit within the multifaceted Jewish world. One good way of keeping in touch with what the Jewish world thinks, worries about, and celebrates is to subscribe to Jewish magazines and periodicals. The following is a list of magazines that you might find interesting. You can either write or call them for a sample (since they all have different slants, approaches, and areas of concern), or ask your local library to get a copy for you.

## Jewish Magazines and Periodicals

*Conservative Judaism*, 3080 Broadway, New York NY 10027, (212) 678-8019

*Jerusalem Post International Edition*, P.O. Box 282, Brewster NY 10509, (800) 955-8559

*Jewish Spectator*, 4391 Park Milano, Calabasas CA 91302, (818) 883-5141

*Judaism*, 15 E. 84th St., New York NY 10028, (212) 879-4500

*Lilith: The Jewish Women's Magazine*, 250 W. 57th St. #2432, New York NY 10107, (212) 757-0818

*Midstream*, 110 E. 59th St., New York NY 10022

*Moment*, P.O. Box 7028, Red Oak IA 51591, (800) 777-1005

*The Reconstructionist*, Church Road and Greenwood Avenue, Wyncote PA 19095, (215) 887-1988

*Reform Judaism*, 838 Fifth Ave., New York NY 10021, (212) 249-0100

*Sh'ma*, Box 567, 23 Murray Ave., Port Washington NY 11050, (516) 944-9791

*Tikkun*, P.O. Box 332, Mount Morris IL 61054, (800) 545-9364

In addition to the books, magazines, and periodicals that deal with various aspects of Jewish life and history, a wealth of creative educational experiences is available through catalogs and publishers of Jewish texts and materials. All of the following sources will gladly send you a catalog or listing of their publications.

**Sources for Educational Material and Catalogs**

A.R.E. Publications, 3945 S. Oneida St., Denver CO 80237, (800) 346-7779

Behrman House, 235 Watchung Ave., West Orange NJ 07052, (800) 221-2755

Central Conference of American Rabbis Press, 192 Lexington Ave., New York NY 10016, (800) 833-0720 Ext. 25 (also for *CCAR Journal*)

Jewish Publication Society, 1930 Chestnut St., Philadelphia PA 19103, (215) 564-5925

Jonathan David Judaic Book Guide, 68-22 Eliot Ave., Middle Village NY 11379, (718) 456-8611

Judaic Media, 453 E. Ninth St., Suite 107, Brooklyn NY 11218, (800) 638-8273

JWB Book Council, Music Council, and Lecture Bureau, 15 E. 26th St., New York NY 10010, (212) 532-4949

Kar-Ben Copies, 6800 Tildenwood Lane, Rockville MD 20852, (800) 452-7236

KTAV, 75 Varick St., New York NY 10013

Torah Aura Productions, 4423 Fruitland Ave., Los Angeles CA 90058, (800) 238-6724

Union of American Hebrew Congregations, 838 Fifth Ave., New York NY 10021, (212) 249-0100

Beyond the books and materials that are available for your personal study and education, the Jewish community has created a wide variety of communal institutions, service organizations, and educational foundations to serve your needs and the needs of your children. Below is a list of most of the major organizations in the Jewish community in the United States, any one of which would be delighted to share its important work with you.

## Jewish Organizations of Interest

Agudath Israel of America (Orthodox), 84 William St., New York NY 10038, (212) 797-9000

America Israel Public Affairs Council (AIPAC), 440 First St. NW, Washington DC 20001, (202) 639-5200

B'nai B'rith Hillel Foundation, 1640 Rhode Island Ave. NW, Washington DC 20036, (202) 857-6560

Coalition for the Advancement of Jewish Education (CAJE), 261 W. 35th #12A, New York NY 10001, (212) 268-4210

Council of Jewish Federations (directory of Jewish Federations, Welfare Funds, and Community Councils), 730 Broadway, New York NY 10003, (212) 598-3500

Federation of Reconstructionist Congregations and Havurot, Church Road and Greenwood Ave., Wyncote PA 19095, (215) 887-1988

Jewish Fund for Justice, 920 Broadway, Suite 605, New York NY 10010, (212) 677-7080

Jewish Peace Lobby, 4431 Lehigh Road Suite 141, College Park MD 20740, (301) 589-8764

Jewish Welfare Board (directories of Jewish Community Centers), 15 E. 26th St., New York NY 10010, (212) 532-4949

Mazon (The Jewish Response to Hunger), 2940 Westwood Blvd. Suite 7, Los Angeles CA 90064, (213) 470-7769

National Conference on Soviet Jewry, 10 E. 40th St. Suite 907, New York NY 10016, (212) 679-6122

National Havurah Committee, 441 W. Carpenter Lane, Philadelphia PA 19119, (215) 438-6108

New Israel Fund, 111 W. 40th St. Suite 2300, New York NY 10018, (212) 302-0066

New Jewish Agenda, 64 Fulton St. #1100, New York NY 10038, (212) 227-5885

Shalom Center, 7318 Germantown Ave., Philadelphia PA 19119, (215) 247-9700

Shomrei Adamah (Guardians of the Earth), Church Road and Greenwood Ave., Wyncote PA 19095

Society for Humanistic Judaism, 28611 W. Twelve Mile Road, Farmington Hills MI 48018, (313) 478-7610

Union of American Hebrew Congregations (Reform Movement), 838 Fifth Ave., New York NY 10021, (212) 249-0100

United Jewish Appeal, 99 Park Ave. Suite 300, New York NY 10016, (212) 818-9100

United Synagogue of America (Conservative Movement), 155 Fifth Ave., New York NY 10010, (212) 533-7800

## A Final Word

Raising Jewish children in our contemporary world is a challenge unlike any faced by previous generations. The rapid pace of change that bruises and batters our very social structure year in and year out, the overwhelming amount of new information, new scientific "facts" that flood the marketplace of ideas each year, and the general breakdown of barriers between ethnic and religious groups all combine to make the task of passing on a Jewish heritage and culture daunting, to say the least.

One of the benefits of being a rabbi is that I have had the opportunity to work with Jews of all backgrounds and inclinations as well as non-Jews who have chosen to raise their children with Jewish identities. Although there are often great obstacles to overcome, and most parents today never feel absolutely qualified for the responsibilities that they have assumed, it is constantly inspiring to see how it truly takes only one dedicated parent to transform the entire family.

Ideally, if there are two parents raising a child they work as a team. Decisions are more effective if mutually supported by everyone involved, and child rearing is always easier when there is consistency within the family. Children need to know what to expect within their home, what their parents' expectations are, not only of their behavior but of how they are to see themselves in relation to others. I hope this book has been helpful in guiding you in the direction of a successful, nurturing, supportive, and consistent child-rearing approach.

It takes the greatest kind of faith to have a child in the first place. It takes faith that the future is not pre-determined by others, that you *do* have a say in the quality of life of your family, that what you do and what you teach your child *do* make a difference in his life. Based on nearly twenty years of watching families of all kinds struggle to raise Jewish children, I *know* that this is so.

Someone once said that making the decision to have a child is to decide forever to have your heart go walk-ing around outside your body. Striving to be the parent you want to become, doing your best to pass on to your child the values and ideals that will help her achieve success and personal fulfillment, is one of the most pro-found responsibilities any human being can undertake.

If this book helps you along your path to that goal, I will feel well rewarded for having written it. In fact, if being in touch with me will help you in this journey, please call or write to share how you are doing. The privilege of being a rabbi is that others let you into their lives in the most significant of ways. It would give me great satisfaction to hear of your progress in creating the kind of environment that empowers you and your family to fulfill themselves and strengthen your spirit-ual, cultural, and religious identity.

I can be reached at Kehillath Israel, 16019 Sunset Blvd., Pacific Palisades CA 90272, (213) 459-2328.

# Glossary of
# Hebrew Blessings

## Shabbat

Upon lighting Shabbat candles:
> Baruh ata Adonai Elo-haynu meleh ha-olam, asher kid-shanu b'mitz-votav vetzee-vanu lehad-lik neyr shel Shabbat.

> Blessed are you our God, divine power of the universe, who makes our lives special through commandments, and commands us to kindle the Sabbath lights.

Before drinking the wine:
> Baruh ata Adonai Elo-haynu meleh ha-olam, boray p'ree ha-gafen.

> Blessed are you our God, divine ruler of the universe, who creates the fruit of the vine.

Before eating the bread, or before any meal:
> Baruh ata Adonai Elo-haynu meleh ha-olam, ha-motzee lehem min ha-aretz.

> Blessed are you our God, divine power of the universe, who brings forth bread from the earth.

## Hanukah

Before lighting the Hanukah lights:
> Baruh ata Adonai Elo-haynu meleh ha-olam, asher kid-shanu b'mitz-votav vetzee-vanu lehad-lik neyr shel Hanukah.

> Blessed are you our God, divine power of the universe, who makes our lives special through commandments, and commands us to kindle the Hanukah lights.

Baruh ata Adonai Elo-haynu meleh ha-olam, sh'asa nisim la-avotaynu, ba-yamim ha-hem baz-man ha-zeh.

Blessed are you our God, divine power of the universe, who performed miracles for our ancestors in days of old at this season.

On the first night only, add:
Baruh ata Adonai Elo-haynu meleh ha-olam, she-he-he-yanu, ve-key-manu, ve-hig-yanu laz-man ha-zeh.

Blessed are you our God, divine power of the universe, who has kept us in life, sustained us, and allowed us to reach this special moment together.

## A Few Blessings to Acknowledge Special Moments in Life

Upon obtaining something new, doing something for the first time, eating the first fruit of the season, or other special time:
Baruh ata Adonai Elo-haynu meleh ha-olam, she-he-he-yanu, ve-key-manu, ve-hig-yanu laz-man ha-zeh.

Blessed are you our God, divine power of the universe, who has kept us in life, sustained us, and allowed us to reach this special moment together.

Upon seeing a rainbow:
Baruh ata Adonai, Elo-haynu meleh ha-olam, zoher ha-brit.

Blessed are you our God, divine power of the universe, who remembers the covenant.
(Referring to the rainbow sign to Noah in Genesis)

Upon hearing good news:

> Baruh ata Adonai Elo-haynu meleh ha-olam, ha-tov ve-ha-maytiv.

> Blessed is the source of divine goodness in the world.

Upon recovery from danger or an illness:

> Baruh ata Adonai Elo-haynu meleh ha-olam, she-gamalani kol tov.

> Blessed are you our God, divine power of the universe, who bestows great goodness upon me.

Upon seeing unusually beautiful trees or creatures:

> Baruh ata Adonai Elo-haynu meleh ha-olam, she-kaha lo be-olamo.

> Blessed are you our God, divine power of the universe, who has such as this in your world.

# Common Questions about Raising Jewish Children

**Q:** *Because we're not really religious, how do we help our child feel Jewish without attending synagogue?*

**A:** I assume by "not really religious" you mean that you don't regularly participate in organized religious services, holiday celebrations and communal worship, and don't necessarily believe in the existence of a supernatural all-powerful Being. Since I understand the term "religious" to refer to the individual's search for ultimate meaning in life (see Chapter 1), you may indeed be religious in the most important sense of that word.

Helping your child *feel* Jewish is a function of involving your child in Jewish activities, experiences, special moments and celebrations. Feeling grows primarily out of doing, so the more you expose your child to positive, enjoyable, nurturing Jewish experiences, the more he or she will develop a positive Jewish self-image. (For more details, see Chapter 3.)

**Q:** *My husband is Jewish and I'm not. Everything is fine until Christmas rolls around—I want to put up a Christmas tree for the children and he does not. Is there a way we can resolve this peaceably?*

**A:** The easiest resolution that many couples have found is to have a tree, but declare that it is *yours,* rather than your husband's tree or the family's tree. In that way, you can tell your children that the tree is a special part of your heritage and past, and you are having it because you are Christian and it brings back wonderful memories of your own childhood.

Children generally have no problem understanding that mommy is Christian and daddy is Jewish, regardless of the specific identity that you may give to them. Your husband can tell them that the tree is a way of celebrating "mommy's holiday" with you. This approach is quite often very successful, even in homes where the children are being raised with a Jewish identity. Of course, overall I believe that religious consistency encourages emotional stability in children, but you will find that if you and your husband eliminate religious tension, it won't exist for your children either. (For details and additional suggestions, see Chapter 4.)

**Q:** *My wife and I are both Jewish, but we live in a community where there are no other Jews and the nearest synagogue is fifty miles away. How can we help our children feel Jewish out here in the country?*

**A:** Obviously you are in a do-it-yourself Judaism situation. Don't despair. Judaism has always been primarily home centered anyway, so you can create a rich, nourishing, active Jewish life anywhere, as long as you search for ways to bring Jewish culture, tradition, ritual and customs into your home. The rabbis of Jewish tradition used to refer to the home as a "mikdash me'at," a "small sanctuary." They felt that every family could bring holiness, sanctity, specialness into their home, through the rituals they perform, the celebrations they share, books they read and attitudes they teach.

Your job is to find resources that will help you to teach your children the fundamentals of Jewish ethics (see Chapter 2 for ethics and 7 for resources), and to bring as many rituals and holiday celebrations into your home as you are comfortable with (see Chapter 3). Another suggestion is to identify Jewish personalities in the news, in movies, recordings or television when you find them, so as to build a sense of positive Jewish pride of association with your children (see Chapter 6).

**Q:** *A friend of mine keeps telling me that it's not possible to raise a moral child without giving him or her a religious foundation and sending him or her to synagogue. I disagree. How do you feel about this?*

**A:** Although synagogues are the foundation of the Jewish community, and probably the single most important Jewish institution ever invented, you don't have to belong to a synagogue to be a good, decent, ethical and moral person. Moreover, you don't even have to be Jewish to be a good, decent, caring ethical person.

Children learn what they live, and what they live is dependent upon you and the model that you set through your own actions. It's more important for your children to see you reaching out to help the poor, the downtrodden and the oppressed, than it is for them to see you go to services at a synagogue. Your actions thunder in their minds much louder than any mere prayer possibly could.

Having said that, it's only fair to acknowledge that the ethics that you do choose to express in your life, the standards by which you measure ethical behavior do stem from a *religious* foundation. They come from thousands of years of Jewish civilization, as expressed in the words of the Torah (the Five books of Moses), the prophets and the writings of the Bible and subsequent commentaries and clarifications over the centuries. To give a child a strong sense of morality *is* to inspire within them a desire to understand the religious foundation from which all ethics sprang (see Chapter 2).

**Q:** *I was horrified the other day when my child came home from school and related to me that a classmate had told him that Jews weren't nice people because they killed Jesus. How do you recommend I handle this?*

**A:** Assuming that your child is of elementary school age, your first response should be to comfort and reassure the child that his/her classmate is *wrong*, Jews *are* as nice and wonderful as anyone else. You might hold your child and say, "That was a mean thing to say, I bet it hurt your feelings."

It is appropriate to let your child know that he/she hasn't done anything wrong, that the other child is at fault for saying something that was designed to be hurtful, and that you are sure that if his/her classmate's parents knew that he/she had said something so mean they would be disappointed and want to know where he/she ever got such a mean and untrue idea.

If your child is curious about Jesus, you might simply tell him/her that Jesus *himself* was Jewish, and a wonderful teacher a very long time ago, and of course Jews didn't kill him. If it were my child, I would actually let her classmate's mother and father know in a friendly, non-intimidating way that their child picked up some undesirable and inaccurate information about Jews and Jesus, and is saying hurtful things to other children (including my own) that you are sure they wouldn't want him/her to be saying.

**Q:** *Last week my children and I were in the mall and they wanted to visit Santa's house, sit on his knee and tell him what they want for Christmas. I told them no because we are Jewish and we don't believe in Santa. They were devastated. I somehow feel that I didn't handle this well. What do you think?*

**A:** Well, I used to visit Santa in the department stores when I was a child, sit on his knee and tell him that I was Jewish so I wanted things for Hanukah and not Christmas. Most of the time, the Santa's seemed to be Jewish too! Of course, I turned out to be a rabbi, so maybe you should watch out. . . . Anyway, I don't think it is a big deal to enjoy Christmas lights, visit Santa's house or help friends and neighbors (or even relatives) trim their trees. That is not the same as "celebrating" Christmas in my eyes, and I think it is easy to make the distinction clear to your children. Very few children really think that the man in the mall is going to magically bring them whatever they want (sorry, they all know it's you or no one), and I have never found "believing" in Santa to be much of an issue (see Chapter 4 for more).

**Q:** *I'm Jewish and my wife is not. We both agreed to raise our children in the Jewish faith, but for her own personal reasons she does not want to convert. The dilemma is this: If I*

*take the children to synagogue occasionally, how do I deal with
the issue that my kids will not be considered Jewish?*

**A:**    According to liberal Jews (both the Reform and Reconstructionist Movements), a child is considered fully
Jewish if one of his/her parents is Jewish and if the child
is raised as a Jew. If you give your children a Jewish
identity, allow them to participate in acts of Jewish identification, like give them Hebrew names, celebrate Jewish holidays, perhaps join a synagogue and allow them
to get a Jewish education, then they will be considered
fully Jewish by a large percentage of the world's Jews.

On the other hand, since the Orthodox and Conservative Movements still cling to the biological definition
of who is a Jew, if they choose to live their lives within a
traditional Jewish framework or move to Israel, then at
some point they may feel the necessity to formally "convert" to Judaism. In general, however, it should be very
easy for you to find a local liberal synagogue that will
accept your children fully as Jews and encourage your
entire family (including your wife even if she never converts) to participate to the level of your own differing
interests and needs (for more details, see Chapter 4).

**Q:**    *My daughter is getting married to a man who is Catholic. I've always looked forward to giving her a large wedding
with all the traditional trimmings. Of course, I want a rabbi
to preside over the ceremony, but her fiance wants a priest. It's
all getting terribly complicated. How do you suggest we resolve
this?*

**A:**    My first piece of advice is to realize that it's your
daughter's wedding, not yours. You already had your
chance to have the kind of wedding you wanted, and
now it's her turn. Your job as a parent is to be support-

ive, loving and non-judgmental regarding the choices that your daughter *as an adult* has made.

It's important to remember, that getting married is the process of leaving one's family of origin (in this case, you) and creating a new primary family with one's spouse. Her primary loyalty *must* lie with her husband, and not with you, your spouse, your other children or the extended family. That is why the Bible teaches us (in Genesis) that when people get married they leave their father and mother and cleave to each other and become one.

I suggest you let go of your own fantasies about her wedding, and find out what *she* wants. That would be the most wonderful and loving wedding present that you could give.

**Q:** *My 16-year-old son has announced his plans to live on a kibbutz in Israel this summer. I have mixed feelings about this—on the one hand I am proud and happy, but at the same time I am frightened for his safety. Should I let him go?*

**A:** Your concern is understandable given all the publicity that Israel gets in the news, and the fact that she is still officially at war with her Arab neighbors. However, I lived in Israel for two years, and send teenagers there every summer to participate in a variety of outstanding programs. It never fails to be one of the most important and moving experiences of their lives, not to mention an excellent process of maturation.

I strongly recommend that you let your son go to the kibbutz; it will be an invaluable lesson in self-reliance and connection to the greater world Jewish community, and the physical dangers are in fact less than walking down most streets in most urban centers in America.

**Q:** *Although my husband is Jewish (I was raised Lutheran) he was not raised with a sense of his own background. I would like our children to have a greater sense of their own background, but, without my husband's help, I literally don't know where to start! What can you suggest?*

**A:** This book is a good place to start, of course, and there are other books and materials on basic Judaism (see Chapter 7). There are also "Introduction to Judaism" courses given in nearly every city in North America, and most local synagogues have classes on raising Jewish children or celebrating Jewish holidays as well.

The best thing you could do is to take a class on Judaism together with your husband. This would not only give you a common vocabulary with which to approach the issues of raising your children with a positive Jewish identity, but would undoubtedly help strengthen your relationship in the process. In the end, although it is obviously much better to have the involvement and support of your husband in your childraising efforts, you can give your children a strong Jewish identity by starting with the simple suggestions found in Chapters 2 and 3 of this book.

**Q:** *My son came home crying today. Another child called him a "kike" on the playground. How can I make it better?*

**A:** This problem is similar to any instance when someone resorts to calling your child names. The most important thing is to point out that unfortunately, throughout life we meet up with people of all ages who say things about others that are just plain mean. Sometimes kids in particular like to hurt other kids' feelings, just because it makes *them* feel better, or somehow superior to put down someone else.

Name calling is a very hurtful thing, and it's appropriate for your child to be upset by it. The word "kike" really doesn't have any meaning to either your child or the child who said it, except to stand for something nasty and negative. Perhaps you can use this as an opportunity to hold your child in your arms, and tell him that too often people are simply foolish and hurtful toward others. Thinking about how awful it feels is a way of reminding ourselves how important it is not to treat others in any way that we wouldn't like to be treated (see Chapter 2).

**Q:** *Are there classes that a non-Jewish parent can take in order to learn more about Judaism without converting?*

**A:** Yes, you will find in every city one or more "Introduction to Judaism" classes either through local synagogues, Jewish federations, Bureaus of Jewish Education or Jewish community centers. All of them are designed to provide non-Jews and Jews alike with a basic understanding of Judaism, whether your goal is conversion or simply expanded knowledge. In addition, you might take a look at the resources listed in Chapter 7 of this book since many of them can provide you with your own private "Basic Judaism" course.

**Q:** *There are so many negative stereotypes about Jews and Jewish behavior, how can I prepare my child to deal with this?*

**A:** There are negative stereotypes concerning just about every ethnic group that exists on our planet. Most of the negative Jewish stereotypes won't affect your child until he or she is at least into the teen years, at which time it is possible to teach a little of the history of anti-Semitism and where these particular stereotypes came from. I have found that a short history lesson on the realities of medieval Europe, persecutions of the Jews by the church and European governments provides an excellent basis for young people to understand and respond to the negative stereotypes of Jews that have been passed down from the past (see Chapter 6).

**Q:** *My husband wants to have a traditional bris/brit for our newborn son. I can't stand the idea of a surgical procedure being performed under non-medical circumstances. How can we resolve this?*

**A:**   In defense of the Mohel (ritual circumcisor) profession, my own experience watching both medical doctors and mohels perform circumcisions is that the mohels have a lot more experience. After all, this is their area of expertise and specialty, and they simply do a lot more of them than most doctors. For that reason, I wouldn't be too concerned about the expertise or professionalism of traditional mohels.

With that said, there may be other reasons for not using one. First of all, an Orthodox mohel will probably not recognize either the son of a non-Jewish mother as Jewish or the son of a mother who converted to Judaism through any means other than Orthodox as Jewish. This means he will bring two other orthodox Jews to the bris and formally "convert" your son as part of the process.

If you have become a Jew by choice with a Reform, Reconstructionist or Conservative Rabbi, a bris with a traditional mohel can turn into an insulting and offensive experience for you. One way to avoid this is to have the surgical procedure done in the hospital, and give the child a Hebrew name at a separate ceremony either in your home or at your local synagogue.

A second way to deal with the problem is to hire a certified Reform mohel. These are medical doctors who have been trained in the religious ceremony as well through the Hebrew Union College-Jewish Institute of Religion. You can find out about them by calling the college at (213) 749-3424.

**Q:** *My Jewish husband and I are an interfaith couple. We are expecting our first child soon, and my Catholic mother says she cannot sleep at night knowing that her grandchild will not receive a Christian baptism. She is convinced that our baby will be condemned to purgatory. Help!*

**A:** There are two ways to approach this issue. First, you can decide that since the baptism is so important to your mother, and is meaningless to your husband (that is, it literally doesn't mean anything; neither making your child Catholic nor indicating anything specific about your childraising choices for the future), that you will make her happy and ease her mind by having the child baptized. I know many interfaith couples who have chosen this option, and have raised their children Jewish, celebrated their Bar and Bat Mitzvahs and managed to placate the strong feelings of everyone to some degree.

Second, you can simply tell your mother that *you* don't feel as strongly about it as she does, that you don't think your child (and by extension your husband and his entire family) will be condemned to purgatory for not being baptized, and that although you still love her just as much, as an adult with your own mind you have chosen not to baptize your child. What you decide depends on how important all this is to you, and whether making your mother happy is more important than any

specific opinions, beliefs or feelings you and your husband might have on the subject.

**Q:**  *The High Holidays are approaching and I would like my*
*son to accompany me to synagogue. "Ah mom," my son said,*
*"who cares about that old stuff?" How can I combat my son's*
*sense of apathy?*

**A:**  The best thing to do is to create a positive, nurturing, happy Jewish environment within your home all
year through the incorporation into your lifestyle of
Jewish customs, rituals, holidays and ethics. In that way,
your children come to value being Jewish for all it adds
to their lives, and getting them to participate in the
High Holidays or any other Jewish activity is not so
difficult.

Of course, Jews of all ages get bored with High Holiday services, the many hours of sitting at prayer, listening to long sermons and even longer chanting of
Hebrew. The trick is to see the High Holidays as an
opportunity to get in touch with the values that are
most important to them and use it to move their lives
forward toward their goals.

Making sure that you aren't just "once a year" Jews
will set a pattern of behavior and identification that will
encourage participation in all Jewish holidays. It might
also be valuable to point out that the ideas, themes and
thoughts that form the center of the High Holiday experience are as relevant and powerful today as at any
time in history. All of us need some time each year to
reexamine who we are and where we are going, what
we stand for and who we want to become. This is the
primary purpose of the High Holidays.

**Q:**  *My son was not circumcised at birth. He is now 12 and is asking about a Bar Mitzvah. Must he undergo circumcision beforehand?*

**A:**  No, not unless he wants to have a Bar Mitzvah in a traditional synagogue (and then it's up to the individual rabbi). Being circumcised, although one of the most distinguishing marks of Judaism for the past 4,000 years, does not *make* a boy a Jew. Neither does it make someone *not* Jewish if he isn't circumcised. I don't know any synagogue that asks boys if they are circumcised, and frankly I doubt that it would really matter to most rabbis. That is a private decision of the family and the son to make. There are many other more public and more important ways to demonstrate Jewish identity and a connection to the Jewish people (including celebrating special life-cycle events such as a Bar Mitzvah), and that is what is really important.

**Q:**  *I'm Jewish and my husband is Protestant. I never cared about religion until I had my first child, and I find that I care much more than I thought. This is causing real problems in my marriage and I'm afraid that the tension will affect the children. Why is this happening and what on earth can I do?*

**A:**  You are suffering from what I call the "time bomb" syndrome. It is like a religion time bomb was set during the time you were being raised as a child, and it has just gone off in your consciousness. The fact is that each of us changes over time as we grow, mature and reach new stages of our own development. The things that are important to you at age 20 seem trivial at age 30, and things that you never even thought of at 25 become all consuming at 35. That's just the nature of life and comes along with being human.

The most important thing to do is talk to your husband about your feelings, your needs, your dreams and your desires. Be open about your feelings, about your rising levels of commitment to Judaism and see how he reacts to that. Perhaps he will be encouraging of your life process and support you in bringing more Judaism into your lives as a family. You might also suggest that you both take an introduction to Judaism class together, which will help your relationship and help him to understand you better.

Of course there are some things in life you simply can't love away, and it might be in the end that you and your husband are really no longer able to live together. It is unfortunate, but it does happen, especially in interfaith marriages. If you can reconcile your differences, see them as gifts from each other to expand your experiences of life you might rediscover all the reasons that you fell in love in the first place. Otherwise, it is better to face the reality of what you need to be satisfied and fulfilled in life now than later in life (see Chapter 4).

**Q:** *Every December my children get all upset when they see the neighbor's Christmas festivities (parties, trees, presents, and so forth). How do I explain to my children that Christmas is for Christians and Hanukah is for Jews? How do I overcome their jealousy for their friend's celebrations?*

**A:** You do it exactly as you think. You say "Christmas is a holiday for Christians to celebrate the birthday of Jesus. It isn't our holiday, so we don't celebrate it in our own home, but we can celebrate it with our friends in their homes as their holiday. We celebrate Hanukah for eight nights instead, and perhaps we can invite some of our Christian friends over to celebrate Hanukah with us as well."

You also tell them the same thing you would say if your child went to someone else's birthday party and then got jealous because the birthday child got all the presents. Children need to learn to share, to recognize that all people are not exactly the same, that each of us has many times when we get the presents, and are the center of attention, but now is not one of those times.

I don't think you need to deprive your child of a wonderful experience, as long as it isn't *your* Christmas celebration. Make sure you get invited to share Christmas with some Christian friends or relatives, or perhaps volunteer at a local hospital to replace Christian workers who would love to be home with their families. This would be the best "Christmas present" you could possibly give your child (for more discussion of this issue, see Chapter 7).

# Index